While [he] was
pronouncing those words
in delivering the cup to me,
"The blood of
our Lord Jesus Christ,
which was given for thee,"
the words struck
through to my heart,
and I knew
God for Christ's sake
had forgiven me
all my sins.

—Susanna Wesley

CHOICE BOOKS
The Best In Family Reading
P. O. Box 503
Goshen, IN 46526
We Welcome Your Response

Susanna

GLEN WILLIAMSON

LIVING BOOKS
Tyndale House Publishers, Inc.
Wheaton, Illinois

Third printing, Living Books edition, June 1987

Library of Congress Catalog Card Number 84-52223
ISBN 0-8423-6691-1, Living Books edition
Copyright 1985 by Glen Williamson
All rights reserved
Printed in the United States of America

To Corinne

CONTENTS

FOREWORD

It was twenty years ago when I first thought of producing a plain account of the spiritual awakening in eighteenth-century England. Since preparation for such a project necessarily required a careful analysis of all the great revivals of the church, intermittent times of study were pressed into a busy schedule. In the process new ideas emerged that completely overshadowed the first one.

Fortunately, I came to realize that another work on the Wesleyan revival would be a rehash at best of that which scores of others had already done. At the same time, my prime interest in renewal underwent a significant change. The situations—political, moral, and spiritual—that immediately preceded the awakenings gained the preeminence.

At the close of the study, any type of treatise

on the Wesleys was put on hold. Several years later when the plan was given serious consideration again, it was not to be a story of the revival, but of Britain's darkest hour just before the dawn.

Susanna is a biographical novel of the mother of John and Charles Wesley. It depicts the time in which she lived, introduces the family she bore, and presents the part she and her husband Samuel played, inadvertently, in the revival that rocked the world for Christ.

Thirty months of intensive research, including a summer in England, preceded the writing of this book. Scores of works from tomes to pamphlets were carefully perused. These included letters written by Samuel Wesley that were discovered as late as 1963. I was determined to get to know Susanna and Samuel as well as I once knew my own mother and father. The Wesleys' amazing strengths, their glaring weaknesses, their unyielding devotion to God, and their intense love for each other that rode out a hundred storms, came under careful scrutiny.

Details have been added to fill in areas left vacant in strictly documented material, and sometimes names have been given to the nameless. To complete a picture, an occasional character has been created. Great care has been taken, however, that every line is kept in character with the personalities, times, and available facts.

ACKNOWLEDGMENT

In reconstructing Susanna's childhood, I am deeply indebted to my daughter, Lorraine, a kindergarten teacher of broad experience with gifted children. Psychologist Margaret Connet, Ph.D., who read these chapters as they were being written, gave valuable advice, especially in analyzing emotions and bringing characters to life. Mrs. Janet Barnes, assistant librarian, Dr. Williams Library in London, answered important questions concerning the Annesley family and graciously granted me the privilege of taking a rare copy of a heavily documented biography of Susanna to America. Bishop Emeritus, Walter S. Kendall, and his wife, Ruth, whose interest in Wesleyana is of long standing, perused these pages as they appeared and gave much needed encouragement. My wife, Corinne, worked closely by my side through long months of research both at home and abroad and later spent countless hours typing the final script. With the help of these and many others, this work was made possible. I could not have done it alone.

chapter **1**
The Annesleys

If Mr. Lacey had a first name, there were few indeed who knew it. He was just plain Lacey to his friends, and he had no foes. Irish by birth, teamster by trade, the little man was untutored but amazingly well read; and he smiled his way into the hearts of all who knew him. Lacey was equally at ease with the rich and the poor, the great and the small. There were hundreds of townsmen who hailed him heartily as he traveled the cobbled streets of seventeenth-century London.

He kept a tight rein on his spirited geldings, a loose rein on his inquisitive tongue—and he learned something important, he said, from everyone who rode his rig. That rig, during the great plague of 1665-66, was as versatile as its driver—available always as taxi, bus, delivery, ambulance, or hearse.

Among Lacey's special friends was Dr. David Isaiah Downie, a man as different from himself as could be imagined. Scores of times Lacey had taken the busy medic on his rounds. And while the two men could find hardly a word or a reason to address each other, nevertheless there developed between them a deep and distinctive kinship. Sometimes silence is more revealing than conversation.

The tall, lean doctor, attired always in conservative grays and blacks, was a dreary sort of fellow of no particular age or color, with a strong Edinburgh accent, and about as emotional as a bagpipe.

It was late in the afternoon of the first day of September 1666, that Lacey reined and tethered his steeds near London Bridge, where he and Dr. Downie had arranged to meet their pastor, the Reverend Doctor Samuel Annesley. For months, the minister and the medic had labored night and day with the sick and the bereaved, pausing only now and then to catch a bit of rest, as opportunity afforded.

The strain was fast becoming more than they could bear. This was the reason for the little visits they arranged through the ever-accommodating Lacey.

London Bridge in those days was a city within itself. It was covered, several stories deep, with dwellings, shops, counting houses, dens of iniquity—everything from best to worst. Its ornate windows, tiny gables, imposing towers, and belching chimneys composed an architectural wonder in seventeenth-century England. The bridge, the only one that spanned the River Thames in London, united the growing metropolis. The city was laced with narrow, sometimes cobbled, streets; and while it was blessed with churches great and small, and boasted of its centers of commerce, it was cursed with the stench of disease-ridden slums infested with vermin—mostly small, black rats.

Poverty, misery, and early death—so long a way of life—enslaved the city's poor, with hope of emancipation entertained by only the very ambitious. And even the stoutest youths, in those years of the devastating plague, were giving up their last vestiges of faith in any change for the better.

History records that seven thousand persons died in a single day when the strange and deadly malady reached its height. Even if this figure were grossly exaggerated, the thought of evacuating the dead—not to mention nursing the dying day after day—staggers the imagination.

It was in one of the better shops near the end of the busy span, that the Reverend Annesley spotted the two companions who had arrived before him. The pastor was a most impressive gentleman—tall, straight, handsome, and, as Lacey once described him, "well put together." He fairly oozed intelligence and grace.

As he approached the table of his friends, Lacey popped up to greet him; but the dreary medic retained both his seat and his solemn composure. He knew that he would be asked again for an opinion on the progress of the fight to end the plague, and he had nothing to give. The limited science of medicine, in which he was well instructed, provided no hint of therapy or drug that might even retard the malady that threatened to annihilate the populace, and Dr. Downie knew it. He was a good man, conscientious, unpretentious; and beneath his solemn, serious exterior was a heart of deep compassion for the poor and oppressed.

Pastor Annesley smiled down upon his somber friend, for he knew him well and loved him as a brother. And, as expected, he asked the usual question: "What report do you have today, David?"

"The people continue to die like rats," the doctor answered without apparent emotion, and it was certain he supposed no one would question his pronouncement. But he must have forgotten Lacey, who was posted and positive in areas far beyond anything expected of men of his humble profession. Suddenly his expressive countenance came to life in reaction to the gloomy report.

"Sure and if what the doc was sayin' is true, it would be a great blessing, don't you know. Ya see, the fact is, if only the rats would die like the people, soon they would be gone and the fever would disappear."

If Dr. Downie resented the little speech, no

one would have guessed it as he turned to the teamster. "Then you really believe the plague is spread by the rats?" he asked seriously.

"Of course," the little man responded. "Every time the hairy varmints get bold enough to bristle up and defy ye right on the street, the fever comes."

"You are most observing," the medic admitted with what Pastor Annesley interpreted as a note of appreciation. "One doctor I know has long identified the plague with the rodents; but, pray tell, how are we to destroy them? Even if we killed off all but a few, the slums are so conducive to their propagation that within a year the pests would number in the hundreds of thousands again."

Lacey looked the doctor straight in the eyes. "Aye," he began with a burst of enthusiasm. "The answer is right in the books, you know. All we need is to give his royal highness a fiddle."

"I see," said the other. "You are saying that if fire would consume the slums of London as it did those of ancient Rome, the city would rebuild itself with decent housing and perhaps some sanitary system of sewage disposal."

"Exactly," enjoined the little layman. "A whole new day would dawn for our city and all of Britain, don't you see?"

"If I remember my history correctly," said the doctor, "the emperor blamed the Christians for the holocaust that destroyed two-thirds of Rome. Surely you don't believe that."

"Aye, but I do, indirectly," Lacey responded without hesitation.

"What do you mean by *indirectly?*" Pastor Annesley asked, breaking into the odd exchange for the first time.

"I mean it was God!" The little man spoke with conviction. "If the Almighty didn't light the first fagot, at least he dawdled along with the distracted emperor while the flames accomplished his purpose."

"Do you mean to suggest that God might start such a fire in London?" the doctor asked.

"Why not?" asked Lacey seriously. "Or, at least, if one started from natural causes, he would stand back and let it do its work."

"Extraordinary," the medic barely whispered.

Pastor Annesley broke into the conversation again. "The plague spreads even as it seems to be receding," he said. "There were three new cases reported last week in Spital Yard. That's my neighborhood, you know."

"By the by, Pastor," Lacey asked with sudden interest. "How is your lady getting along?"

"My wife?" asked the pastor. "I've been away for the past three days. She was all right when I left her. Why do you ask?"

"I'm sorry." Lacey was apologetic and concerned. "I didn't know. You see, yesterday I was driving in the area and I saw your pretty lass, Judith. She said her mother was sick and had taken to her bed."

"My God!" cried the pastor, coming to his feet. "The plague." The outburst was not profane, but an earnest petition. "Come, David, Lacey will take us in his rig."

Such a ride over the cobblestones neither of the passengers had ever experienced before. In the shortest possible time, Lacey reined up his horses near a square brick dwelling in Spital Yard, the comfortable home of the Annesleys. Seconds later, the pastor was pounding on the door as Lacey and the doctor came puffing up the steps to join him. The door swung open. There, in apparent good health, stood Mrs. Annesley, happily welcoming home her husband and his friends.

"Thank God, you're up," the pastor cried as he embraced her warmly. "We heard you were sick. Tell us about it."

Before she could respond, the man of medicine took over, motioned the lady to a chair, and laid an experienced hand on her forehead.

"You don't seem to have a fever," he reported.

"No, Doctor," she answered. "I was ill this morning, but I'm all right now."

That evening, Mr. Lacey, relating the incident to his wife and son, smiled broadly and said, "The ol' sawbones niver changed his expression, but I tell ye, I saw a twinkle in his eye, I did. Then he asked the dear lady if it weren't so that she had been sick the morning before as well. And she gave him a bit of a smile—understanding like—and said, 'Yes, Doctor. I think I have had this same sickness every year of my married life.'

"Then I looked at the pastor and, good husband that he is, he was grinning as though he had just led a whole flock of sinners to the p'int of repentance."

Mrs. Annesley quietly instructed the servants to fix a hot supper for her husband and the doctor, and to prepare the guest room for the latter, whom she had invited to spend the night. The pastor's house and table were always open to friends and strangers alike. Hundreds of Londoners had tasted the hospitality of this "queen of the manse," as the lady was often called by students of her husband's school and members of his growing congregation.

The Annesleys were not poor people. Moderately wealthy, they enjoyed most of the advantages reserved for London's more affluent citizenry; but, wisely, they made no show of opulence. Servants were kept in the background. Since most of the visitors who came to the door were students and ministers, struggling for an existence, no servant was allowed to answer the summons. This friendly gesture was the responsibility of the mother or one of the older children.

Notwithstanding the annual pregnancies, plus the tears Mrs. Annesley had shed with her husband over more than a dozen small white caskets, she remained a slender, delicate lady of grace and gladness. There was about her a mature sort of beauty, enhanced by soft wrinkles that framed her sensitive mouth and clear blue eyes. Warm and inviting, her contagious smile flashed freely at the slightest provocation. She liked people, loved her husband, adored her children, and worshiped her Savior without hint of reservation. Mrs. Annesley was a saint of God.

When bedtime came that evening for the younger children, she called her family and their guest together for meditation and prayers. Dr. David Downie, who seemed always at a loss for words, amazed the family as he led them in earnest supplication. He petitioned the Throne of Grace for mercy upon the scores of souls who in that very hour were entering eternal realms. The good man became eloquent, begging for strength and wisdom that he might minister more effectively to the physical needs of unnumbered patients who looked upon him as their only hope. His prayer became more fervent when he launched out in sincere intercession for Pastor Annesley and his colleagues as they carried the message of salvation to a lost and dying generation right in their own community.

The doctor paused for breath, but his prayer was not finished. Beginning again in lower voice, he tenderly beseeched the great God of heaven to keep his omnipotent hand upon the children of this pastor's household. He asked that they might grow in grace and knowledge, to become great in the eyes of heaven, reflecting the love and devotion of their godly heritage. Raising his voice again, he held before the throne the gracious mother of this excellent family, upon whose narrow shoulders had been laid so great a burden. Then he concluded, "Jehovah God, we thank thee for the gift of so many mothers' love through the generations, by which you have blessed this world, and without which Adam's race would have passed away in centuries past. . . ."

When the good man finally voiced his last amen, the family, kneeling at their chairs, remained in awed silence. The pastor and his lady, holding hands, wept softly as the doctor became his somber self again.

It was little Judith who finally broke the silence. Laying a tiny hand on the good man's arm, she looked up into his eyes and stated firmly, "I'm glad you came and prayed tonight. I'm scared."

The other children reacted nervously; and the mother, who never failed to understand and comfort their childish emotions, ushered her brood to their beds, whispering words of faith and courage.

It was four o'clock in the morning, while all the house was deep in slumber, that Pastor Annesley was awakened with a start at a loud, determined pounding on the outer door of the residence. He knew instinctively that terrible tragic news awaited as he lighted a candle, grabbed a robe, and started down the long stairway two steps at a time. The ominous, incessant banging on the door continued.

"All right! All right," he cried. "I'm coming."

Across the imposing corridor, into a narrow reception hall, he sped. It was not until the aggressive caller heard him struggling with the heavy iron bolt that held the great door against the dangerous London night, that he ceased his incessant knocking. Then the door swung open.

In the dusky light of the early morning, Pastor Annesley recognized Lacey, who was already shouting the message he bore.

"The fire!" he cried. "My God, the fire! It will take the city. Hurry! There isn't a minute to waste."

Then Dr. Downie appeared, attired in a long, loose nightshirt that had been loaned him by his host. His usual calm demeanor was completely gone.

"Doctor," cried Lacey, "I hoped you would be here. I want to tell you I'm sorry, I am, for what I said about God wanting the city to burn. I didn't know it would be like this."

"Never mind," the medic answered. "I agreed with you, you know."

"We'll be with you in a minute," the pastor promised; and moments later, the men were on their way. Saving souls and saving lives had long been the burden of their existence; this was merely another chapter.

Criers had been alerting the people from the outset. Lacey and others who were equipped to be of special assistance in evacuating those trapped by the blazing inferno were called out early.

The fire was reported first in Pudding Lane near the bridge. A strong northeast wind was spreading the flames; flying fagots filled the air, and all hope of controlling the blaze was abandoned forever. The dry, timbered buildings, turning into fiery furnaces, were already taking unnumbered lives. Wooden dwellings, most of them several stories high, stood in such close proximity that the streets were too narrow to accommodate horse-drawn wagons.

Dr. Downie and the pastor had been ministering in one of these areas for weeks, and there it was that Lacey left them. As the two men stepped down from the rig, they heard wailing cries of helpless souls, and up the narrow lanes they ran. Mothers and their tiny tots received their first attention, and they led or carried scores of them through the terrible heat to points of safety. All through the day they pursued their unselfish labors, work for which heaven alone would someday reward them. At home, Mrs. Annesley spent the day preparing sacks of food and jars of water to be carried by her older children to the faithful volunteers who fought for lives in the flaming inferno.

By nightfall the raging fire was approaching Queenhithe on the riverbank and had reached northward to Cannon Street. From their father's study at the top of the great house, the Annesley children gazed at the glaring spectacle that pushed the darkness back miles into the English countryside. Their father had not yet returned, nor had they expected him. He would give to the last ounce of his extraordinary strength, and they knew it.

For three dreadful days the fire raged. It reached the Royal Exchange. Guildhall and the custom house were destroyed, and it burned its way westward until St. Paul's Church burst into flames. By then the fire seemed to have finished its work of destruction, and the wind fell during the night. The fourth day laid bare the area of disaster, with only patches of fire remaining. Eighty-nine churches, and more than thirteen thousand homes, in addition to all else along three hundred streets, had yielded to its irresistible onslaught. Untold grief and despair were left in its wake. It reached into the Annesley household the second night when the father, nearly exhausted, limped up the steps to report that Dr. Downie had fallen in harness, a child in his arms.

Later, at the burial, during Pastor Annesley's eulogy, Mr. Lacey wept unashamedly, as did little Judith and her younger sister.

But the long-range view was brighter. Lacey's opinions had not been as far afield as they had seemed in the heat of the holocaust. The great plague, already receding, died to be sure. And eventually, new, wide thoroughfares lined with decent houses evolved out of the disaster. Thus the way was paved for the great metropolis of London to become one of the largest, most important cities of the modern world.

Three years later the reconstruction program was well underway. And while prosperity was still in the distance, a new spirit of optimism had developed in the people.

Dr. Annesley's congregation was growing, as was his family. So it happened that one warm spring afternoon in 1668, the good pastor, returning home from his many labors, was met again at the door by his adoring wife.

"I'm afraid I have some news, Samuel," she said with a hint of a smile. "I have been terribly nauseated the past couple of mornings."

"Not again, my dear," he answered. "I'm sorry. I had hoped. . . ."

"It's all right, Samuel," she said. "I've borne many. If the Lord wills that we have yet another, it will be all right. Perhaps this one will be the greatest blessing of all."

The child she carried would be her last. They named her Susanna, called her Sukey, and she soon became the idol of all the family.

chapter 2
"No, Papa"

Susanna might have been forever spoiled. She was the prettiest child of an unusually beautiful family. And, being of a serious nature, she seldom needed reprimanding. The older children adored her, catering to her every whim. She was her mother's baby, of course, and the unbounded delight of her indulgent father.

But the tiny tot did not spoil easily. It was said she rarely cried except for exercise. She seldom smiled and almost never laughed. Even so, she was not of an unpleasant disposition. The line between prodigious and highly intelligent is hard to draw, but Susanna must have been more than the latter term suggests. At two and one-half, she was learning at a level the older children had not attained until they were five or six. Several of them became her faithful tutors.

The alphabet she conquered quickly; and before she reached her third birthday, she was counting to one hundred. By then, her thirst for knowledge was clearly asserting itself.

"What comes after hundred?" she begged of Judith.

Judith was busy with her own studies and didn't want to be bothered. "You start over again," she answered, not unkindly. "Hundred one, hundred two; that's all there is to it."

So she left her little student to work out the problem for herself, and work it out she did to the best of her ability. "Hundred seven, hundred eight, hundred nine," she whispered, but where to go from there she didn't know. Always before, when she reached the number nine, there was a larger number waiting to be learned and memorized. So Susanna tugged at Judith's arm once more.

"All right," the older girl gave in reluctantly, "what is it now?"

"What's the next big number after hundred?" she asked.

"Thousand," Judith answered. "Now please let me read."

Susanna went back to her private study. "Hundred eight, hundred nine, *thousand*," she counted proudly. Then she went on, "thousand one, thousand two," but when she eventually came to thousand nine, she was stumped again. She thought of Judith, but decided it would not be wise to bother her anymore. Her mother was resting in her favorite chair, so she went to her.

"What's the next big number after thousand?" she asked abruptly.

Mrs. Annesley smiled her prettiest as she reached down to pick up her ever-amazing little daughter.

"I guess the next big one after thousand is million," she said, "but don't you worry about it. You should have no need of a number as large as that for a long, long time." She kissed her baby's cheek. The child registered neither objection nor response. Susanna had important studying to do and sitting back in her little chair, she kept practicing.

"Thousand eight, thousand nine, *million*," she repeated until she had it well in mind. Then she launched out, "Million one, million two . . . ," but when she came to million nine, she decided to rest her study in higher mathematics until some other time.

Later she heard her father coming in from his labors. She knew his routine. He would kiss her mother, wave to whatever children were in sight, then hurry to his study at the top of the great house to work on next Sunday's sermon. Susanna waited until he had ample time to reach his desk; then she hurried up the flights of stairs to invade his private domain. Busy as he always was, he never disappointed her. She was certain he never would. As she approached his chair, she extended her arms, asking to be placed upon his lap. As always, the maneuver was successful.

"I love you, Papa," she stated simply. It was

to him only that she openly displayed affection.

"Well, now," the father began, "what has my brilliant little scholar been learning today?"

"Counting," she answered.

"Still learning to count, aye?" he asked. "The last time I checked, I believe you had reached fifty. How far can you count today?"

"Million nine," she answered simply. "To-morrow, I'll go on from there."

Try to imagine his reaction. It was no greater, though, than one he experienced several days later, when Susanna came tripping into his private sanctum again.

"Papa," she cried. "I know the alphabet."

"Well," he answered. "What's so exciting about that? I heard you recite the alphabet months ago, and recently I heard you can count to a million nine." He smiled broadly.

"Oh," she explained soberly, "I have that all straightened out now."

"I'm sure you have." He smiled again. "But what's so wonderful now about your knowing the alphabet?"

"I mean in Greek," she stated proudly, and proceeded to rattle it off from Alpha to Omega. How had she learned it? Earlier, Judith, with her father's help, had nearly mastered the Hellenic tongue. And now she had been teaching the letters secretly to her little sister.

Such was Susanna at the tender age of three.

Dr. Samuel Annesley was a Dissenter, a noncon-formist. In the early 1660s, he and a large number of Church of England pastors, including such men as Richard Baxter, Daniel Williams, and Bartholomew Westley and his son John, had suffered ejection from their pulpits. In short, they had chosen, for conscience' sake, to forego the security of their *livings,** rather than to bow to the demands of the established church. They proceeded to form independent societies, asking the Lord to help them live on the Sunday morning collections. Soon these dissenting congregations were loosely bound together to form a fellowship embracing, for the most part, Luther's doctrine of salvation by faith. The movement was strongly Presbyterian, and, at first, quite evangelistic.

Samuel Annesley had been rector of St. Giles, the largest Anglican congregation and one of the most beautiful churches in London. His salary of seven hundred pounds annually had been handsome, too, especially when many pastors were forced to feed their families on fifty pounds or less. He owned the spacious residence, four floors in all, in Spital Yard near Bishopsgate; and, while Susanna was still a child, he was pastoring a church of no less than eight hundred Presbyterians. The people had erected a new sanctuary, complete with pulpit and pews and three large galleries, and it was there he preached until his death in 1696.

The load was heavy. Not only was Dr. Annesley serving a large congregation, but he had been

---

Living is the Anglican term for pastoral appointment.

chosen by his dissenting brethren to oversee the work of all the pastors. This constituted a superintendency with heavy responsibilities; and if he had not had exceptional ability in organization, it would have required undue time and travel. What he did instead was open his home to the brethren for counsel, and there many important meetings were held. This placed the burden of travel upon the men.

Hence, both pastors and leading laymen became well known to the Annesley household, and the children were happy when the visitors allowed their own youthful offspring to accompany them. Sarah, Elizabeth, Judith, and Anne, all in adolescence, quite naturally took special interest in the boys who came. They studied each one with wistful, cautious glances, hoping and praying that some beautiful relationships might develop—but only sober, steady, spiritual-minded fellows were considered by any of them.

Then there was Danny. When Susanna was five, she took an abiding interest in this lad who was nine years older than she, simply because he was an excellent storyteller. She was not alone. All the young people sat gladly at his feet when he was in a storytelling mood.

"Is Danny's father coming to the meeting tonight, Papa?" they would ask, and as often as not the answer was yes. Anxious also was Susanna's sister, Anne, who had caught the lad's eye, and she his.

Danny was a great admirer of Dr. Annesley,

and he planned to follow in his steps. The boy believed his call from God was to be a pastor. From the moment he announced his intentions, he was looked upon with growing favor by Susanna's older sisters—Anne in particular. And since they were among the prettiest, best behaved, and most learned of all the girls in London, his interest in them also caught on quickly. Danny was barely fourteen, a full year younger than Anne; but being tall and mature for his age, he appeared to be at least a couple of years her senior.

It was tiny Susanna, though, who never failed to amuse him as she listened with wide-eyed interest to every detail of the yarns he spun. And he couldn't help but notice that she never laughed when a bit of humor brought howls of delight from the others. He liked her as big boys tend to like their little sisters.

There came a temporary break, however, in the rather strange relationship that developed between them. It happened when Susanna first learned the lad's full name: Danny Foe. To discover the meaning of every word she encountered had become an obsession with her. All words fell into two simple categories: those she liked, and those she detested. One day, the term *foe* kept popping up. So she asked her brother Benjamin what it meant, and he gave the word its strongest connotation.

"Foe means enemy," he said. "One who hates you, wants to harm you, even kill you. Sometimes," he went on, "a foe is one who pretends to be your friend until he gets a chance to hurt you."

The little one shuddered. *Foe* suddenly became a word she hated with all her heart. Then by accident she learned that this was Danny's name, for she heard someone call his father Mr. Foe. Two evenings later, Danny was in the home again, and Susanna flatly refused to listen to his stories or even remain in the room where the other young people had gathered. Danny was unable to understand her aloofness, and no one could give him an explanation. Judith and Anne questioned her, but Susanna wouldn't talk. She wanted nothing more to do with Danny, that was all there was to it.

As usual, her father was the one who solved the riddle. When he questioned his little admirer, she related the whole story.

"So," he responded as casually as possible, "you think the boy's name makes him some kind of a devil, aye?"

"It does," she answered.

"No, Susanna," her father spoke with great earnestness. "The name never makes the person. The person makes the name. Sometimes good, sometimes bad. Danny is a good boy, and he makes the bad word good. Do you see?"

She sat with her chin propped in her hands, elbows on her knees, as she slowly contemplated his words of wisdom. They made sense, she decided, and that was all that mattered.

"I'll listen to Danny's stories again," she stated

simply. Then she left her father's study and, without a word of explanation to anyone, resumed her place at the feet of the enthusiastic storyteller.

All this was finally explained to Danny, whose only response was that he didn't like his name either, and someday he would have it changed. Whether he remembered the incident is not known, but it is a matter of record that in 1703, he did indeed have his name changed to Defoe. And as Daniel Defoe he was to become known to all the world as teller of the tale *Robinson Crusoe*. Later, Daniel decided against the ministry, became deeply involved in the politics of the day, and developed into a prolific writer.

Although his romance with Anne Annesley failed to develop when he was sent away to school in Newington Green, yet throughout his colorful life he remained a close friend of the family. After Dr. Annesley's death in 1696, he wrote an elegy calling him "the best of ministers and the best of men."

During the next three years, Susanna was quietly, busily rounding out an elementary education. Actually, she was reading at college level by the time she was eight. And it was at that tender age that she became sorely bothered by an important social problem which centuries of enlightenment would only partially resolve. After mulling it over as an alert teenager might have done, she took her case to her father.

"Papa," she said, coming directly to the point.

"Why aren't Judith and Elizabeth going away to school like Benjamin and Danny and the other boys?"

Dr. Annesley, deeply absorbed in some dry divinity, failed to realize how important the question was to his little girl. Without raising his eyes from the page before him, he answered simply, "Because they are girls."

"But why can't girls go to school?" she asked, forcing him to face the issue.

The problem, of course, was not new to this minister whose thinking was years ahead of his time. Slavery, workhouses, child abuse, the oppression of the working classes, women's rights—all these and much, much more had long been subjects of his most serious concern. And his brilliant protege, Daniel Defoe, at seventeen was already writing papers dealing with sex discrimination, thereby getting himself into trouble. Dr. Annesley could debate the issues with the best of scholars; but how could he explain these deep-seated problems to an eight-year-old girl, even if she were a prodigious youngster? His burden for the moment was simply to set her childish mind at ease.

"You see, daughter," he began slowly, "girls are expected to learn to care for children, keep house, prepare meals, and wash clothes—while boys equip themselves to earn a living for their families when they grow up and get married. That is why boys are sent away to school, while the girls are allowed to stay home with their mothers."

He glanced down at the child who, in characteristic pose, sat with chin in her hands, elbows on her knees, her large blue eyes looking into the depths of his soul. He squirmed a little but wasn't sure why, for he was certain he had made his point.

"Now you understand, don't you, dear," he concluded.

Nothing moved but her lips.

"No, Papa," she said.

chapter **3**
"Yes, Papa"

It seems that the Annesleys embraced a middle-of-the-road position in regard to instilling their religious beliefs into their family. Without making tough demands, the pastor and his wife were objective in their teaching of fundamental truth. And although some of the children later stepped off the parental path, their disappointing decisions created no rift in the family, and the problems were always left with the Lord.

Susanna, who had just turned nine, continued to reject the doctrine of salvation by faith, and she abhorred hypocrisy. However, her determination to keep every commandment, to *work out her own salvation with fear and trembling*, grew stronger. Earlier, she assumed that her father and his colleagues who had been ejected from their Anglican pulpits were right, and the rest of the world was wrong. She further assumed that the dissenting ministers, without exception, walked the narrow path from which she knew her father never strayed. After all, he was their leader, their chief pastor—their *bishop*, even if they didn't use the term.

But Susanna became disillusioned. One of the pastors who often sought out Dr. Annesley for counsel and prayer was being brought before him to answer charges of immoral conduct. Susanna, whose sense of right and wrong was amazingly well established, was suspicious of any knowledge that came in whispers; so she made her way to her father's study to get the story straight from headquarters.

"Yes, daughter," he said in answer to her query. "What you heard is true. The tempter is strong and deceitful, you know, and sometimes God's children are weak and yielding."

"But, Papa, a Christian is one who is Christ-like. You told me so yourself. How can one who is not a Christian be one of your pastors?"

"Oh, I didn't say he was not a Christian, Susanna. I remember the day he accepted Christ as Savior, right in our Sunday morning service. You see, Satan doesn't leave us alone when we become Christians."

The good man paused. "Doesn't Satan tempt you sometimes?" he asked.

"Yes, Papa," she answered. "But I tell him no, and he believes me."

The pastor was silent. He had to concede that his little daughter did exactly as she said, better than anyone he had ever known.

"Papa," she went on with a hint of hesitation,

"do you remember when you became a Christian?"

"No, Susanna," he answered slowly. "I must have been very young, for I can't recall a time when I didn't know my sins were all forgiven."

The girl turned and left the room. It was as though she had said, "Thank you. I have no further questions."

Christian parents may be slow to detect flaws in a child's comprehension of spiritual truth. Instead, a sister or brother may be the first to recognize those shortcomings, and it was so in Susanna's case. Even at the tender age of nine, she was dogmatic in her theology. To walk as uprightly before God as before her earthly father was her firm commitment. This, she believed, was the only way she could finally merit admission to a mansion in glory—and she had no intention of missing that.

Susanna was a stubborn girl. When she heard her father preach that only through the atoning blood of Christ could one become a child of God, she brushed the sentiment aside. It was Elizabeth who sensed her sister's need of someone to redirect her thinking. She decided to shoulder the responsibility herself, although she knew it would not be easy. (After all, how does one convince a younger sister who lives a nearly perfect life that she isn't right with God?) Elizabeth prayed sincerely for a proper time and place to bear effective witness.

So it happened that on October 20, 1679— one of those chilly, foggy mornings well known to Londoners of every generation—she and Susanna marched up the steps to the heavy gothic doors of their father's church. It was the Lord's Day, which, to these devoutly religious daughters of the manse, was both sacred and serene. As always, the gaping entrance reminded Susanna of the portals of heaven. In that moment Elizabeth dared to ask her sister if she enjoyed the inward witness that she was a child of God.

"Susanna," she asked, "have you been saved by grace through faith; not of works, lest one might boast?"

"I walk in the light," the girl retorted. "I am determined to live so well that when I die, God will have faith in *me*. I feel safer that way."

"I understand," Elizabeth answered kindly, "but if you would only accept the Lord Jesus as your Savior, you would be certain of your salvation now. You would feel something truly wonderful. Can't you believe that?"

Susanna's mind was closed; and so it would remain for a long, long time.

The two girls, having arrived several minutes late, stood at the back of the crowded auditorium searching in vain for places to sit. Toward the front, to the right of the sanctuary, Mrs. Annesley sat as always with her children. She had tried to save places for Elizabeth and Susanna, but two Quaker ladies had entered the church ahead of them and were already moving into the empty seats. Then the girls were spied by Mr. Lacey, the little teamster who sat with his wife and son at the end of a pew. He motioned to them and asked his wife to make room for the pastor's daughters. The lady, being large and strong, did as her husband suggested, unceremoniously accomplishing what no usher would have dared to try. The startled people made room for the girls, but the seat was uncomfortably crowded. So Lacey smiled down at Susanna and whispered, "If ye don't mind sitting on my lap, Sukey, we can make a mite more room, ya know."

Susanna responded favorably with neither smile nor frown, and the arrangement proved to be an excellent one. An unrehearsed drama was about to unfold at the front of the church, and this placed her in a position to watch—near enough to Lacey's right ear to ask him what it was all about.

The service had hardly gotten underway when one of the Quaker ladies rose and demanded an opportunity to speak. The pastor waited in silence as the woman in black proceeded to call down the wrath of God upon the startled congregation.

"What's happening?" Susanna asked.

"It's Elizabeth Bathurst," Lacey whispered. "She and her sister used to be members here. It isn't that she doesn't have respect for your father, but some things have developed in the church which she doesn't like. I guess that's why she joined the Quakers."

"Oh, I remember her," Susanna answered softly. "She's a fine lady, and the Quakers are good people. Why did she leave?"

"Listen to what she is saying and maybe you will find out," Lacey suggested just as the woman's piercing proclamations began to rise in pitch and power.

Then, at a signal from Dr. Annesley, the enraged woman was confronted by a couple of "elders" who asked that she hold her peace during prayer time, wait until after the benediction to voice her protests, and remember she was in the house of God. Apparently the gentle rebuke reached her sensitive soul, and while Susanna was unable to hear her quiet response, she felt certain it included a soft, sincere, *"I'm sorry."* In any event, the woman resumed her seat in the pew with Mrs. Annesley and her children.

The service continued without further interruption. The pastor refused to allow the outburst to disturb him visibly, and he was at his best that morning in the pulpit. Susanna, as always, was proud of her parent. But her pride received a resounding blow at the close of the service when she saw Miss Bathurst and her sister being ushered out the door. It was apparent that the assurance of being able to voice her sentiments after the benediction was being denied.

"That isn't right, Mr. Lacey," Susanna solemnly spoke her mind. "I'll talk with my father about that this afternoon."

"Sure and wouldn't I like to hide in a closet and listen," the teamster answered with a hint of a smile.

Later, when Susanna went into her father's study, she found him sitting at his desk, a veritable picture of despair. He motioned her to a chair.

"Sit down, daughter," he said. "I know why you're here and what you are about to say. So I may as well go ahead and try to answer your questions before you ask them.

"I want you to know that under God I have done my best, but it isn't good enough. Our cause is crumbling, our church is no longer the spiritual temple it used to be, and I don't seem to have the wisdom and strength to repair it. Factions keep forming and heresy runs rampant among us. I try to keep it hidden. That is why I couldn't allow an old friend to voice her sentiments this morning. She didn't know it, but she would have defeated her own purpose as well as God's if she had continued; and, of course, our church would have suffered greatly."

Susanna was listening well. "Doesn't God have an answer to all these problems?" she asked.

"Yes, my dear, but God is never in a hurry. His plan is so much greater than ours, so universal, so far reaching, that we can't comprehend it."

Susanna was perplexed as she left her father's study. She didn't know who or what was right or wrong. This may have been the reason she became more and more dogmatic in her position that only obedience might enable one to be justified in the sight of a holy God. She made her way to her room and knelt beside her bed.

"Dear Lord," she prayed, "I want to help you. I have come to make some new and better promises. So, for every hour I spend playing or reading stories, I will spend another hour in prayer and Bible study. I promise. Amen."

Such honest but radical vows, made under emotional stress, are common enough, heaven knows. But they are seldom kept with the same wholeheartedness that produced them. And God understands. But Susanna never allowed this to become her problem. Sixty years later her son, John Wesley, was to write in his journal concerning the teaching he received in childhood:

> I was carefully taught that I could only be
> saved by universal obedience, by keeping
> all the Commandments of God; in the mean-
> ing of which I was diligently instructed.

Susanna was nearly twelve when she accepted the invitation of an older girl to attend a meeting of a Socinian society. This liberal, Unitarian group was made up of former members of both Anglican and dissenting churches.

"We think you will like us," Susanna was told. "We are free from all that silly dogma we used to suffer under. We believe in God and let it go at that. Isn't he the important one after all?"

The people seemed contented, which was greatly to Susanna's liking. She also felt that here was a culture into which she might project her own theology of obedience. She could see it was sorely needed. She felt like a missionary among such liberal "Christians," so she continued to attend their meetings. And while she maintained her own distinctive life-style—nothing could change that—she calmly adopted their teaching. To her, God was an old, long-whiskered man upon a celestial throne, smiling down upon the universe, hoping his children would obey him.

By this time, Susanna, who was maturing early, could pass for one well into adolescence; intellectually, she could easily hold her own with college students of any level. She was still the prettiest of all the Annesley children, and she remained the same serious, self-righteous, congenial daughter of the manse. Not once did she suggest that any of the family accompany her to the Socinian meetings, nor did she try to justify her decision to become a part of what her father called "the great heresy." As always, she appeared neither happy nor distressed.

Elizabeth, who had always felt responsible for her younger sister, was groaning beneath a burden of guilt for having failed her. She blamed no one but herself, and the pressure was fast becoming more than she could bear. At that point she took the problem to her father's study.

"Elizabeth!" the pastor observed with deep concern. "You look as though you might have come face to face with Lucifer himself. Tell me your troubles. Perhaps I can help you."

"It's Susanna," the girl cried, fighting tears and trying to keep her composure. "Not one of us dares to argue with her—she's that strong, you know. She always has an answer for everything, and since no one can criticize the way she lives, how can anyone help her? I'm worried, for I know that I'm to blame. I failed her. She has never really been happy. Never in my life have I heard her laugh. And as she gets older, I sense a certain sting in her words when she's displeased, a crispness that seems to say, 'Watch your step or I'll put you in your place.' She loves you, Papa, more than anyone. Can't you show her how wrong she is in going with that Socinian crowd?"

"No, my dear. All I can do is pray for God's will to be done. I have the same problem with Sukey that you have. Your mother and I have discussed it, sometimes on our knees, but neither of us believe that confronting her will accomplish anything. We have to trust that her good sense will win her back."

Dr. Annesley smiled. "If she were old enough to marry, perhaps some young pastor could win her love and change her mind."

"No, Papa. Sukey will never marry. Men like to dominate their women, you know, and where in all England is there one who could compete with her?"

The good man nodded his agreement. He knew that Elizabeth had characterized her sister well. But Susanna was special to him; nothing would ever change that.

"You will never be bothered with her problem, will you, Elizabeth?" Dr. Annesley smiled again as he spoke. "I've noticed how friendly you and

John Dunton have become. Do you wish to talk about it?"

"Yes, Papa. John is a good man, and we have been discussing marriage. He'll be talking with you about it soon."

Elizabeth lowered her eyes and, for several moments, studied the pattern in the carpet. Then she faced her father bravely and asked, "You will not object, will you, Papa?"

"No, daughter. John will have my consent whenever he asks for it," the good man responded. "And someday if a man equally as fine asks for Sukey's hand, I'll grant that too." He paused. "Oh, you said no man would ever want her, didn't you? We shall see."

And that very night, John Dunton, Elizabeth's suitor—a friendly, optimistic, rather eccentric printer who had recently joined Dr. Annesley's congregation—came to visit, bringing a friend along.

The fellow was eighteen, partly Irish and showing it. He was a ministerial student at Newington Green, the Dissenters' school where both Dunton and Daniel Defoe had formerly studied. His name was Sam Westley. Sam had a sense of humor which never failed to make him popular; but he must never have kissed the Blarney Stone, for flattery was not to be found among his many talents. He was too honest for that. Dunton introduced him to Elizabeth and a half dozen other young people who were engaged in a game at a large center table, and Sam proceeded to smile his way into their good graces. Then Susanna, wearing a dress as blue as burning sulphur that matched her eyes exactly, came slowly down the open stairway with her sister Anne. As usual, the young one neither smiled nor frowned, and no stranger could guess whether she were pleased or bored.

Elizabeth quickly introduced Anne, the girl who had once smiled prettily at Danny Foe across that very table. Then she turned to Sukey. "This," she said, "is my youngest sister, Susanna. She is twelve." It was obvious that Elizabeth had good reason for divulging Sukey's age.

Sam was impressed, and natural honesty asserted itself.

"Sukey," he said, "you are a beautiful girl. I hope it doesn't make you conceited."

Susanna was struck dumb, probably for the first time in her life. No one had ever spoken to her like that before, and the young man added to her chagrin by turning his attention again to the others. She wanted to retort, saying that he was the rudest, most despicable man she had ever met, but she held her tongue. She wasn't sure she could handle his response.

Minutes later, when the game took an exciting turn and the players were giving it their rapt attention, Sam addressed the girl again: "It's nice to have one's parent for a pastor," he said. "My father was a minister too. He died two years ago; he was only forty-two. You must be proud to see your father in the pulpit every Sunday."

Susanna rose to the occasion. Instead of giving

him the bashful smile of a little girl which he might have expected, she looked him full in the face and stated firmly: "I no longer attend my father's church. I have joined the Socinians."

She felt certain that would stop him, but all it did was rouse his Irish temper. "You ought to be ashamed," he said, not too unkindly. "I can't imagine an intelligent girl like you, a daughter of so great a Christian as your father, being that stupid."

That did it. Susanna left the room without a word. She needed time to control her emotions, but she was determined to return and face her adversary. She was not about to admit defeat. Minutes later she came down the stairs again, this time to march directly into battle—to defend herself against an enemy who seemed to have forgotten, if indeed he ever knew, that war had been declared.

"You called me stupid," she snapped, "giving me every reason in the world to be angry and hurt. I think it is time you know that for several years I have been reading my father's books, I have a working knowledge of Hebrew and Greek, and I have kept pace with my brother in the study of mathematics. I keep all the Commandments, and I believe in one omnipotent, omniscient, omnipresent God who rules the universe."

"Well," the young man responded, "I'll have to admit that *stupid* was hardly a proper term to characterize an apparent prodigy. You must be aware, though, that the *one God* you refer to is a Trinity, three persons in one Godhead, each with his peculiar office to fulfill. I happen to know that the Socinians deny that."

"And you," she retorted, "should know that the term *Trinity* does not appear once in either Testament, or even in the Apocrypha. It was coined by men."

"Ah, and you should know," he answered gently, "that I am glad it is not to be found in the Bible, for it might be misinterpreted. As it is, the meaning of the term is spelled out again and again. In the Gospels alone God is referred to as Father more than eighty-five times; at least twenty times as the Son; and twenty-five as the Holy Ghost. Jesus put the three together when he said, 'Go ye therefore, and teach all nations, baptizing them in the name of the Father, and of the Son, and of the Holy Ghost.' It is plainly taught that the Son reconciled the Father to Adam's race; the Holy Ghost moved holy men of old to prophesy; and it was the Son who redeemed fallen man through his sacrificial death on the cross. And you must be aware that the Holy Ghost is the omnipresent Spirit who awakens lost souls to their need of salvation.

"And that isn't all. . . ."

"Never mind," Susanna answered meekly. "You have made your point."

Several days later, without a word of explanation to anyone, Susanna quietly took her place in the family pew at her father's church.

During the weeks that followed, Samuel Westley made regular visits to the Annesley home where, on every occasion, he and Susanna entered into theological debate. Between the visits, Sukey buried herself in her father's study, preparing her mind, if not her heart, for the next confrontation. She continued to keep her own counsel, talking with no one, not even her father, about the fiery discussions in which she and her good-natured adversary were constantly engaging. Elizabeth, looking on and occasionally listening in, agreed that both were growing intellectually from the sessions. But she had serious reservations regarding any further spiritual benefit that Susanna might be deriving from them. Always pessimistic about her sister, she shared her fears with her father.

"I've come to talk about Sukey again," she told him. "I'm afraid she is developing a dislike for Samuel that borders on hatred. She is so intense, so determined to prove him wrong, that she could destroy herself. Can't you help her, Papa?"

The pastor responded gloomily. "I'm aware of what you are suggesting, Elizabeth. Yes, I will try to talk with her today."

That afternoon, returning home from his labors, Dr. Annesley made his way as usual up the flights of stairs to his study. There he found Susanna deeply engrossed in a mammoth tome, one that dealt at great length with church organization, polity, and liturgy, that even he considered altogether dry and boring. Actually, it had been years since he had looked between its covers. But it gave him an excellent opportunity to probe her thoughts and engage her in what turned out to be a most amazing conversation.

"It doesn't seem natural," he said, "that you should detest young Samuel so deeply. After all, he is a fine, brilliant lad who loves the Lord and serves him diligently."

"I don't detest Samuel," she answered frankly, as once again her deep blue eyes appeared to penetrate the depths of her father's soul.

He met her telling gaze for one long moment; then he stammered, "My, my daughter. Do you mean to tell me you love him?"

Nothing moved but her lips.

"Yes, Papa," she said.

chapter **4**
The Westleys

The name John White, in seventeenth-century Britain, may have been as commonplace as John Smith is in twentieth-century America. If so, it helps justify a most remarkable coincidence. Early in the 1600s, there were two John Whites in southern England who possessed a number of admirable qualities in common. One, a lawyer of unusual ability and a strong advocate of Puritanism, became a member of the Westminster Assembly of the Divines, an important parliamentary post. The other, a city official of Dorchester, was appointed assessor to assist the first chairman of that highly significant assembly. Each John White had a daughter of uncommon intellect and exceptional beauty. While one of the girls had probably reached her twenties before the other one was born, both were to marry ministers of Dissention.

The older of these girls became the wife of Dr. Annesley and mother of Susanna. The other, whose home was in Dorchester, south of London, met and married a most popular minister, John Westley. Westley was in sympathy with the Dissenters, but he served an Anglican congregation in nearby Winterborn-Whitchurch. Like all the Westleys, he was small of stature with an Irish wit and general good nature that stood him tall among his fellows.

The marriage was a happy one; but the troubles between the Dissenters and the Church of England soon destroyed the tranquillity of their home. In the summer of 1661, less than two years after their magnificent wedding, John was arrested for no greater crime than refusing to use *The Book of Common Prayer* in his church. This had always been a point of controversy between the two factions. For this offense he spent a brief term in jail then returned to his charge, where his people stood firmly behind him. It was the following year, under the Act of Uniformity, that he, along with many other nonconforming pastors, was ejected from his pulpit. Few men have been loved as much and suffered more than he.

It wasn't in character for the good-natured little pastor to give way to depression, as he was possessed with more than ordinary grace and poise. But being forced to leave the people he loved, to give up the work God had called him to do, and to lose his living—his pastoral appointment—in an hour when times were extremely hard, was more than even he could handle. His good wife, however, who was about to present him with their first child, was more philosophical than he about the uncertain future.

"It's all right, John," she said. "God is still in charge, you know. Now forget your troubles and prepare a farewell sermon that will bless the souls and break the hearts of the scores of friends you have made at Whitchurch."

She paused for his reaction; but out of his misery, no word came.

"John," she snapped. "You can do it! You know that, don't you!" Thus she startled him to attention.

Looking into her loving eyes, he managed a smile. "Sure, and you know it too," he said. "In fact, I already have my text."

The lady sighed her relief. "Whatever text you have chosen, John, will be perfect for the occasion. Tell me, how does it read?"

The little man drew himself up, put on an exaggerated air, and recited with great earnestness, "And now, brethren, I commend you to God and the word of his grace."

He did indeed use the text—and that sermon may well have been John Westley's greatest triumph.

The baby, a boy, came in November. John, notwithstanding the sting of his ejection from the church he loved, saw his son baptized before its altar and christened Samuel.

During the next five years, three more children—Timothy, Elizabeth, and Matthew—were born to the Westleys. But only Samuel and Matthew survived infancy; and they were reared in abject poverty due to constant persecution, hard times, and poor management.

At one time, when the family had no place to live, a friend provided them a house, rent free, and John ministered among the Dissenters when opportunity afforded. It was said he went about daily doing good, and finally became pastor of a small congregation. But by then his health was broken. He died when he was forty-two, leaving his family without visible means of livelihood. Samuel was sixteen; Matthew, several years younger. The boys loved their mother and, sensing her predicament, proceeded to assist her in whatever ways were opened to them. With their help and that of loving friends, the good woman was able to manage. But poverty and privation stalked their steps and hunger never ceased to haunt the tiny house they called home.

The younger lad, unable to take this humble way of life in stride, vowed that someday he would study and prepare himself for one of the lucrative professions, amass a fortune, and enjoy the better things in life he saw around him. And Matthew did indeed eventually become a successful doctor.

Samuel, we know, had little in common with his ambitious brother. He was small, witty, and personable, cast in the mold of his father. He made friends easily and always adored his parents, accepting without question the hardships the family endured as a way of life in the ministry. Except for a fiery temper, which he must have inherited from some other ancestor, he walked in his father's footprints. While still a lad, probably as he listened to his father preach, he suddenly became aware of an inward witness that he, even he, was a child of God.

Less than a year after his father's death, Samuel, who had never doubted his call to the ministry, was unable to find employment. It was then that a friend, who saw great potential in the young man, offered to loan him enough money to enroll in Stepney Academy to begin his training. This he accepted as providential; and at the school, Samuel found deep satisfaction in debating current issues with his fellow students. In this he excelled. It was through this experience, and with the help of the headmaster, Edward Veal, that he found he could make badly needed money by writing.

Mr. Veal explained, "If one wishes to be published, he must write what the publisher wants." And one publisher, wanting to promote the cause of Dissention, gave Sam a subject that, with the help of his friend, he studiously developed. Out of it came a caustic piece of sarcasm in which he openly denounced the leaders of the Church of England. The article was published; Samuel got his money; and, pressed by the aggressive headmaster, he proceeded to write more in the same sardonic vein.

It was then that he found himself in trouble. Smarting pricks of conscience began to disturb him, for his good sense told him he was violating his own scruples and naturally meticulous nature. But, needing the money, he tried to justify himself, contending that since the church had treated his father badly, he was only doing his duty. It didn't work.

He faced a strange dilemma. Since he was barely seventeen, he knew he lacked the strength to oppose openly the friendly Mr. Veal, who had so graciously helped him. He knew also that he could not in good conscience continue the writing. But before any decision had to be made, the problem resolved itself. Edward Veal was arrested for his attacks on the Church of England and, soon after, dismissed from the school. Samuel, being so young a student, was only mildly reprimanded for his involvement; and out of the painful experience emerged a militant, feisty, wiser, and extremely honest defender of the faith.

Throughout his life, Samuel could be depended upon to stand foursquare by what he believed to be the right. And more than once, only his remarkable sense of humor kept him out of trouble.

On the advice of friends, he transferred to Newington Green, the Dissenters' school that both John Dunton and Daniel Defoe had formerly attended. His funds depleted, he decided to write poetry to pay expenses. Like many beginners who get a tiny taste of success, he had gained an inflated opinion of his literary ability; but a half dozen rejections seem to have corrected that. He was still trying, though, when Dunton—who was soon to be apprenticed to a busy publisher—discovered him. Young Westley had what Dunton needed: jingles—not poems— *jingles*. And Sam was turning out some pretty good ones. Elegies, epitaphs, and other types of made-to-order verse were in vogue; and affluent families celebrating special occasions paid Dunton well to furnish them.

So, with money trickling in again, Samuel was able to give himself to his studies. He did well academically, but a marked spiritual decline in the school deeply disappointed him. Budding dissenting preachers were breaking rules and living worldly lives that offended Sam's keen sense of propriety. His honest convictions regarding ordinary moral precepts and Christian discipline were being violated severely; and he soon became the militant leader of those conscientious students who agreed with him.

It can be safely said that Samuel Westley was always prudent without being prudish; law abiding but hardly legalistic; and extremely uninhibited while woefully devoid of tact. Socially, he knew no middle ground. He was either accepted with open arms or detested with a vengeance.

It was when the Socinians began to make inroads on campus that Samuel found it impossible to contain his righteous indignation. And when one of its exponents had the audacity to ask him to translate some of the works of John Biddle— sometimes called the father of the movement in

Britain—Sammy's Irish temper broke its bonds. He became the personification of Peter, ready to lop off an ear if necessary to make his point. The frightened offender escaped with both his ears intact, but not until a vociferous Sammy had filled him up to running over. In no way would Westley have a part in denying the sacrificial death of Christ upon the cross; he would gladly shout it's truth from the housetops. Is it any wonder he spoke so sharply to Susanna Annesley on the occasion of their introduction?

John Dunton was a strange fellow. His sense of humor was such that he would often laugh when his fellows saw no joke, and remain completely dead-pan while others howled with glee. He sometimes accepted pieces for publication that no other editor would read beyond a paragraph, and often his judgment proved the better. He seemed to sense what particular piece of prose or poetry would be prized and paid for, and he succeeded where many others failed.

Daniel Foe had taken a liking to John Dunton the day they met at Dr. Annesley's church on Bishopsgate. They were the same age and, on the surface, this appeared to be all they could claim in common. And while Danny laughed at Dunton's eccentricities, the two became inseparable friends while they were students at Newington Green. For a number of years following graduation, they made it a point to meet at a popular coffee house near the campus whenever they were both in London, and it was there John introduced his old friend to a new one, Samuel Westley.

Sammy was nearly four years younger than his companions, but being both an excellent student and an ardent debater, he had no difficulty engaging in their earnest discussions. Mostly he listened, though, for he was well aware that information gained from others with scholarship and experience can be the most inexpensive and effectual route to a liberal education. For more than a year, the three friends met regularly, and while Danny and John remained staunch dissenting laymen, Samuel secretly began to question both the doctrines and practices of nonconformity. It was at this time that John Dunton invited Samuel to accompany him to the home of the Annesleys.

From that day, Samuel seldom allowed a week to pass without paying a visit to the great house in Spital Yard to engage in further theological discussions with Susanna, whom he called, "The Prodigious Daughter of the Manse."

It was in the course of those discussions that Samuel and Susanna discovered a strange compatibility in their developing convictions. More than once when Susanna spoke her mind regarding some point of controversy, Samuel would respond with honest enthusiasm: "Those are my sentiments exactly."

They both abhorred the high Calvinism which theoretically characterized the Dissenters. On the other hand, the corrupt political and moral conditions disgracing the Church of England were even more distasteful. If there had been a third party, one that embraced their Puritanical and theological positions, they would have become its most ardent supporters; but to start such a movement was not in their thinking. They familiarized themselves with both sides of the arguments that had led to the infamous ejection of 1662, in which both their fathers had suffered greatly. And, notwithstanding family loyalty and filial love, they calmly reached their decision. From a purely academic viewpoint, Sammy and Sukey were forced to favor the established church. For one thing, they loved its liturgy. To them, the well-designed service lent dignity to the worship of God; and the orderly, sometimes awesome, atmosphere it created made them feel religious, determined to live by their strong convictions.

But in implementing their plans, there were problems. They needed counsel—the unbiased, detached, impersonal view of someone with an open mind and broad experience who would listen to them and help them choose the right course.

"Aye, but my dear Sukey," Samuel sighed at the hopelessness of finding such a friend to share their thoughts. "The people we know who are knowledgeable in the matter already stand firmly on one side of the fence or the other, ready to present 'irrefutable' arguments which you and I have covered recently—and probably more thoroughly than they have. The question is an old one: to whom can we go?"

"I know of one such person, Samuel," she said. "I should have thought of him before."

"I presume you refer to your father, Sukey. Do you think we dare approach him?"

"My father is always approachable," she answered, "but he is not the one I have in mind. Father tries to be fair, but he has been so deeply involved in this everlasting quarrel that his prejudices are as unbreakable as they are understandable."

"Who then is this scholar you suggest?" Samuel asked.

"He is hardly a scholar in the general sense," she answered. "But in his own right he has earned the title nevertheless. He is an old friend of the family, an untutored, self-educated man with uncanny insight; a little white-haired teamster with an Irish brogue. His name is Lacey. I think I would trust his judgment beyond that of anyone I know. I will see that he is here when you return next week."

And that was the way it happened. Lacey listened to their story without projecting even a question—until the youthful students finished recounting their reactions to every argument, every contention held by either faction in the endless controversy. Then he spoke.

"It's amazing you are," he began, "to have peered so far into problems that the wisest of men have failed to resolve. Years ago, my good friend, Dr. Downie, and I agreed that in the great dispute, both parties were right and both were wrong. We were members at St. Giles, Sukey, when your father was ejected from that greatest of pulpits; and we went with him, for we loved him dearly and knew his heart was pure. I didn't know your father, Samuel, but many times I have taken your grandfather, Bartholomew Westley, to visit his patients after he turned to the practice of medicine. It is a matter of record that both he and your father were dismissed from their livings along with Dr. Annesley and hundreds of their dissenting clergymen. And to this day, unfortunately, the names of Annesley and Westley are numbered with those who are despised in High Church circles. This will be something for both of you to remember when you seek to join the fold, as I can see you are going to do.

"It is no small decision you are making, for you will be turning your backs on a great host of friends as well as your families, and this is a cost ye must be counting.

"This will surprise you, I'm sure, but my advice is for you to go ahead with your planning. You are strong—very strong—both of you. And your influence for good and for God will have a much broader field for penetration in the establishment than in the loosely knit churches of Dissention. And God surely knows both of them need a smashing revival.

"Now I have one question. How do you think

your families will accept your decision?"

Susanna was first to answer. "My father will be hurt, of course, but he knows I will not desert him—only his church. He faces lonely days, for Mother is not well and, except for me, his few remaining children will be leaving the nest he so wonderfully provided for us. He will stand by me: I'm sure of that."

Samuel was next. "My life has been much different from Sukey's," he said. "My mother is poor. She has known nothing but poverty from the day she left home to marry my father, but she is a brilliant lady who loves the Lord and enjoys her religion. She will be terribly disappointed when I tell her I am joining the Church of England; but I can hear her say, 'Do what you must, son, and do your best. God bless you.'

"My grandfather," he went on, "would probably disown me, but he is old and frail. Recently he has taken to his bed, and I have been alerted to expect word of his death at any time. His greater interest has been in my brother, who is beginning his study of medicine.

"My worst fear is whether the church will accept me, for I have helped defame the name of Westley by writing some rather nasty articles about church leaders. Actually, I was only trying to earn money. My plan now is to enroll at Oxford this fall, if I can gain admission. I have decided to drop the "t" from Westley. I think it will be wise to alter my name."

Lacey smiled. "Sure and it is plain to see you

both have counted the cost to the smallest far-
thing. There is nothing left for me to say except,
the Lord bless thee and keep thee . . . and give
thee peace. Amen."

chapter 5

"No, Sukey"

Susanna was finding it hard to concentrate on the book she had borrowed from her father's study. Church bells from towers across the city were ringing, and the day was not the Sabbath. This could mean only one thing—a public execution. Some poor, unpardoned person, refusing to keep step with Britain's ever-changing power structure, was being forced to pay with the gift of life—and the whole world was being invited to witness it.

The fate of the unfortunate one was not all that disturbed the passionate heart and mind of Susanna. She was aware that, even then, hundreds of Londoners were hurriedly fixing lunches to be eaten on grassy plots in plain view of the horrid proceedings. To her, the contention that public executions were a deterrent to crime (and provided needed diversion for families rich and poor) was altogether revolting, nearly nauseating. A strange sense of desolation enveloped her—body and soul. She shuddered to think that fathers and mothers with all their impressionable offspring would, within the hour, be "enjoying" the spectacle. She was glad her father had never allowed his family to leave the house on these awful occasions, and that he instructed his sexton never to join in the bell-ringing.

Added to her burden was the knowledge that the unfortunate one might be a teenager such as herself, who would soon haltingly approach the axe or the noose, only to be bolted into eternal realms. And, according to her unbending philosophy, the next world would be either infinitely better or devastatingly worse than this one, depending entirely upon the victim's adherence to the laws of God.

Both her sympathy and her depression deepened as the incessant clanging of the bells continued to penetrate the silence. Susanna was a sensitive girl, but she seldom failed to control her emotions. This day was an exception. She wept as she sat alone in contemplation.

Perhaps God, in his own time, she mused, *will send forth a great and mighty leader who shall spark a crusade to right the wrongs of the nation and reach to the ends of the world.*

For the first time in her life, she found herself believing—really believing—that such a reformer might make his appearance. The thought, of course, was in no way original with Susanna.

Often her father had voiced the same sentiment; and she had heard her friend, Sam Westley, beg God for revival.

"Send a man," he had cried. "One who will stir the conscience of our commonwealth and put an end to vice and corruption."

As might be expected, Susanna's hero was different from the one her father and Sammy visualized. Hers was a knight in shining armor astride a great white stallion. In her mind's eye she watched him bandy a glistening sword in the sunlight to defeat the powers of evil. In a beautiful epic of peace and promise, she could see his keen sense of justice reward the gentle, and place evildoers in the squalor of their own dark dungeons. Then, dismounting, he would hide his armor away in some secluded closet and become a kindly king who loves his subjects and his queen. Thus he would merit the respect and adoration of the world. In that world, she believed, love and devotion would outshine sin and Satan, suffering and sorrow, degradation and despair. Then perhaps the people would calmly, gratefully, embrace the disciplined life she had made her own from the time she was a tiny girl.

She knew Sammy would not agree with her concept of change. She remembered how, in one of their earnest discussions, he had said, "No, Sukey, the great Deliverer has already come. What the world needs now is an *inward witness* of his presence. The man for the hour will ride a horse, perhaps, for how else could he reach the people? But his sword shall be the Word;

and his only protection, the whole armor of God."

She had hoped he was right, but to her practical, disciplined mind, it could never be. She hadn't argued the point with Sammy. She had merely stated, honestly and firmly, "I am determined to serve Christ and his church with all of my strength, to the best of my ability, as long as I live."

The peals from the towers suddenly ceased. The silence was as shocking as the clamor of the bells had been, and Susanna dried her eyes, still thinking of Samuel. He was then in his fourth month at Oxford and she longed to see him, to hear his voice, to listen to his laugh, to enjoy the twinkle in his eyes. She loved him. She had never told him so, for he had never asked her, and he was too naive to guess it. After all, she was barely fourteen and he was twenty.

It was true that, upon occasion, feelings of special affection for her had entered Sammy's mind, but he had dutifully dismissed that as carnal and dangerous. Susanna had sensed this— as the female mind is prone to do—and it only deepened her devotion. Hers was not the infatuation of a young girl. As Lacey had once said to John Dunton, "That remarkable Susanna was *niver* a young girl." John had agreed.

Susanna's love for Samuel was genuine, eternal—but only she and her father knew it, and she was desperately lonely. She took a letter from the pocket of her tunic and read it carefully, as she had done at least a dozen times before. Sam had written her a warm, friendly note, strictly academic. He wrote about his studies, his roommate, his professors, his ambitions; and, in closing, he mentioned how much he missed "those interesting discussions we used to have." He had signed it, "Your friend, Sam."

To Susanna, the letter said, "Sukey, I like you," leaving her longing for the stronger verb. *It will come*, she promised herself, *I know it will come*.

A heavy rap on the outer door startled Susanna to attention. This was one of the few times in her life, when she had been alone in the great house. Her father had taken her ailing mother for a ride in the country; her two brothers were away at school. Anne, Elizabeth, Judith, and Sarah were at their father's church engaged in duties assigned to them by their pastor/parent; and the servants had been dismissed for the day.

Sukey approached the great barred door with caution. Drunkenness, robbery, rape, and murder were rampant, even in broad daylight, in seventeeth-century London.

"Who's there?" she called.

"Tom Dangerfield," came the answer. "I've come to see Sarah. Is she home?"

Tom was disliked by everyone in the family except Sarah. This older daughter of the manse was bashful and not as good-looking as her sisters. She had never succeeded in making friends or attracting men; so when Tom, likewise awkward and shy, took an interest in her, she responded in kind. Under these circumstances, no one, not even her father, had discouraged Sarah—although the relationship was not to his liking. Dangerfield had not been numbered with the young men who frequented the Annesley household, for he was not a Dissenter. Rather, he was known as a stern, dogmatic advocate of the established church. There were rumors that he was one of the hated informers who were spying on both Catholics and Dissenters, reporting evidence of any unlawful activities to the archbishop. The former Declaration of Indulgence, which had granted freedom of worship, had been revoked; and the present crusade was purely political, mercenary, as stringent fines were being imposed upon violators.

Susanna, always abreast of anything old or new in ecclesiastical circles, identified Tom with Saul of Tarsus, who persecuted the early Christians (and may have called *them* dissenters), stopping at nothing to crush the offensive cult. She was aware that Tom looked upon her as a colleague since she had joined the Anglicans, and she hated the thought of it. *Surely,* she reasoned, *there must have been good Pharisees who strongly disapproved of Saul and his methods, and maybe even his motives.*

"Sarah is not at home," she shouted.

"Open the door," he begged. "I have news that should make you happy."

"No, Tom," she answered. "I cannot let you in. It would be improper, for I am alone. Anyway, you know I disapprove of the activities in which you and your friends engage. Leave now; I will tell Sarah you called."

The young man, angry at the stinging rebuke coming from one whom he considered a child, pounded the door and screamed his displeasure. Susanna went calmly back to her study. Thomas Dangerfield left in a huff.

Later in the afternoon, Dr. and Mrs. Annesley returned to the house in Spital Yard. Susanna unbolted the door and assisted her frail mother to her bed. The good woman was physically exhausted from the long ride and visibly shaken by the day's infamous celebration. She was nearly delirious as she haltingly related the morbid details to Susanna.

She told how a ragged, hungry boy, barely in his teens, had unlawfully set a snare and caught a rabbit on a "gentleman's" estate. For that small misdemeanor, he stood trembling on the ugly gallows that balmy autumn afternoon. While she and her husband, as always, carefully avoided sight of the hanging, their rig was inadvertently held up by a gang of the poor lad's friends who were trying to console his mother. Weeping and wailing, the distraught woman was pleading with God to take her too.

"I know I shouldn't relate these awful things to you, Susanna," she concluded tearfully, "but I have to share them or they will drive me mad."

"I'm sorry, Mama," the girl responded sadly. "It's too bad you had to see the wretched woman."

"Oh, no, Susanna. I'm glad we saw her, for now your father will be sending Lacey to her with money and provisions and words of peace in a language she can easily understand. Your father will go later, but right now the dear woman doesn't need a minister as much as she needs a friend."

Susanna bent down and kissed her mother's cheek. "You shouldn't be talking, Mama," she told her. "You need to rest. I'll leave now so you can sleep." Then she straightened the covers, smiled, and quietly left the room.

A few moments later, she sat alone with her father. She told him of Tom Dangerfield's brief visit, recalling the unpleasant conversation through the securely bolted door, and telling how he had left in anger.

"You did well, my daughter," the pastor responded. "You could hardly have handled the situation better; but there will be trouble and there is nothing we can do to avoid it. Informers like Tom have been entering the homes of some of our ministers, accompanied by specially appointed constables. In their heartless arrogation, they search for anything of value and levy fines for no greater offense than preaching the gospel, and that without recourse."

His lips trembled; Susanna thought he was going to cry. Suddenly she was filled with remorse. Bitter feelings of guilt poured into her troubled mind until she believed that she alone was responsible for all their troubles—her father's mounting burdens, her mother's waning strength, and for Sarah, who, starving for affection, had given her heart to one who didn't deserve a remnant of her tender smile. She thought of Sammy, only to believe that he would never return her love. Nowhere, in that dark moment, could she find even a tiny ray of light in the murky shadows.

Her father, always alert to human frailty and capable of interpreting well the emotions of others, recognized at once the danger signs of depression. The dismal countenance he studied was not in character with the strong, determined, intelligent daughter he knew so well and loved so dearly.

"This has not been a good day for any of us, Sukey," he reminded her kindly, "but we must not let it defeat us. God's great plan is progressing even though we do not understand it."

For a long moment, he studied her carefully. "Is there anything I can do or say to help you?" he asked.

"Tell me, Papa," she answered softly, and again her deep blue eyes were fixed upon him, "why have you not been angry with me for joining the Anglicans?"

He rewarded her with a tiniest hint of a smile. "I learned long ago," he said, "that God and his grace are not limited to any organization or excluded from any fellowship. Christ died, not for groups of people, but for individuals who seek him wherever they may be. You see, Sukey, your mother and I will always love you as our daughter, and respect you as a person who must make her own peace with God. Nothing will ever change that.

"There is something else I must tell you," he continued. "We Dissenters would be in much deeper trouble than we are if it were not that some of our greatest men have returned to the Church of England without dissipating our friendship. They, and other open-minded men who never left the established church, are pleading now for a policy of tolerance toward us. It will all work out in time, but we cannot expect that to protect us when Tom Dangerfield does what I suppose he deems his sacred duty."

"If only I hadn't angered Tom." Susanna's voice was barely audible, and heavy with woe.

"Don't blame yourself, daughter. That, too, may be part of the divine plan. I meant it when I said you could hardly have handled the situation better."

"You are very kind, Papa," she whispered.

The following morning, Tom and the constables came—ransacking, ravaging, tearing through drawers and cupboards—threatening, demanding, cursing; expressing no hint of remorse or apology as they obeyed their orders from someone they had probably never seen. They left the house in shambles; the mother on the verge of collapse; the father speechless and worn; the girls angry and confused. But the worst was yet to come. Elizabeth, bounding down the stairs, screaming, was waving a letter she had found on her older sister's bed.

The message was clear. Sarah and Thomas Dangerfield had stolen away at the height of the din. Something of the real Sarah came through, though, in the closing sentence of the brief, terse note: "I promise, Papa, we will be duly married before night falls."

Without a word, the good man turned and slowly made his way up the open stair without facing his loved ones. They watched him as he grasped the rail. Never had he appeared so weary and bent, so sad, with an air of hopelessness about his sagging shoulders.

"He wants to be alone," Anne whispered to the others.

Susanna watched him closely as she fought to contain her tears. She had never felt so needed in all her life; and with that conviction, a sense of untapped energy surged up to sustain her. Whatever spirit of depression had lingered from those awful hours of the past two days dissolved in the heat of this energy. She knew instinctively that she alone could help her father; but she waited until he had time to get settled in his study, exactly as she had often done when she was a little child.

She found him seated, his face buried in his trembling hands; and she thought she heard a sob as she appeared in the doorway.

He didn't move as she sat down in a chair to face him. Carefully she placed her elbows upon her knees and her chin in her hands, reenacting scenes she was sure he remembered.

"Papa," she said in an almost commanding voice. "Look at me."

Slowly he raised his head to meet the penetrating gaze of her deep blue eyes.

"I have come with a message," she said.

Holding his eyes steadily upon her own, he squared his drooping shoulders. He looked as though he were going to speak, but no words came.

"This has not been a good day for any of us, Papa," she stated firmly, "but we must not let it defeat us. Stop blaming yourself. God's plans are progressing, even though we do not understand them."

As he recognized his own words of the previous day, the muscles around his mouth and eyes relaxed visually. He continued to meet her gaze.

"I love you, Papa," she went on. "So do hundreds of others who will need your strong leadership in the days ahead. They have no one else but you." She paused.

"Tell me, Papa, are you going to let them down?"

With that the good man's strength returned. He arose resolutely to his feet and closed a fist.

"No, Sukey," he said, *"never!"*

chapter 6
Perfectly Proper

Samuel Westley was a veritable picture of despair. He sipped a cup of tea that his angry Aunt Aggie had reluctantly brewed and set before him, but his usual Irish wit was far beyond his reach. His mother, reclining on a couch in the adjacent room, was weeping softly.

Aunts are always much more or much less tolerant than are the mothers of this world—especially when they happen to be included in some fiery family fracas. And it was clear that Aggie's aggravation was barely under control.

"You've hurt your mother deeply," she snapped. "There she lies, crying her eyes out, and *you*—the only one who could heal her broken heart—you sit there as stubborn as an ox! Why don't you go and tell her you are wrong, *dead wrong,* and get this silly, senseless notion out of your head!"

Samuel made no reply. Anything he might say would add fuel to the fire, and he knew it. He had just delivered the astonishing news that he was about to join the established church. He had gone on to say, too, that as soon as he could collect some money owed him by Mr. Dunton, he planned to walk the eighty miles to Oxford, to enroll in his father's Alma Mater.

"Yes," his aunt had fairly screamed, "your father's *school* and your father's *church*—but that was before he was treated like dirt and dismissed from his living! Now you talk glibly of returning to both; you are about to disgrace the name of Westley, and you don't even care."

"No, Aunt Aggie," he had answered. "The name of Westley will remain unscathed. I will not be using it, for I'm having it altered to Wesley as soon as I can."

It was at that point that his mother had left the room. Her weeping soon ceased, however, and she returned, drying her eyes as she stood in the doorway. She was neither as strong nor as bold as her sister; but this time she ignored the opinionated Aggie and calmly addressed her son.

"Samuel," she said, "I was a bit shocked, of course, by your unexpected pronouncement; but we can forget that now.

"Your father loved the Church of England, especially the congregation at Whitchurch where he was serving when you were conceived. It's true that there were troubles; he was ejected and deeply hurt, but it was all over by the time you were born. Son, you remind me every day of your father except that, unfortunately, he lacked your militant spirit. If he were here today—and you'll never know how much I wish it—he and I would agree that you must walk in the light of your own convictions, and together we would give you our blessing. As it is, I shall have to do it alone."

Aggie grabbed a shawl and stomped out of the little house, leaving the mother and son to discuss the future without her.

"Aggie will be all right, son. Don't worry about her. I wish I could help you—it takes money to go to Oxford—but I can barely keep food on the table. Without Aggie and the small compensation she receives, we couldn't live here at all."

"I know, Mother," Samuel responded softly. "As soon as I am ordained and Matthew completes his study of medicine, we will be able to provide for you as Father always wanted to do."

"Thank you, son," she said. "Now I'll help you pack your things."

The road to Oxford was rough and long, and rides were almost nonexistent. Occasionally wagons moved in either direction; but since a sturdy footman like Samuel traveled at about the same pace as the horses, he saw only those he met along the way.

Sam was happy. He had never learned to worry, and the fact that he was entering Oxford with only forty-five shillings in his pocket did not disturb him. He reasoned that while his assets were small, his debts were smaller. He had been able to satisfy his creditors, for John Dunton had paid him especially well for the last epitaphs and "poems" he had written. Also, John had assured him of a continuing market for his work, which would give him at least token assistance with his expenses at Oxford. His fondest dreams were coming true.

The first four months at the university were hard. Sam applied himself to his studies and worked at menial tasks to earn a few pence. Finally, through the help of a professor who appreciated his diligence, he was employed to tutor an occasional student who needed special assistance. There were nights when he went to bed hungry, for he was too proud to mention his need to the well-fed students around him.

Then one evening, sitting alone in his sparsely furnished room, he laid aside his books to pray, to thank the Lord for his goodness and help. Sam was lonesome for his old associates in London and, as usual, his thoughts turned to Susanna. For weeks he had wanted to write to her; but since she was so young, he wondered how her family would react. A letter might suggest to them that he had fallen in love with the pretty girl of fourteen—he, a college man going on twenty-one, and so poor he often missed a meal. What interpretation would Sukey herself place upon such a missive? And what if her father should write back, demanding an explanation? How could he assure him that his interest in

Susanna was purely platonic, that of an older brother or teacher?

Then the lonely student asked himself just what his feelings really were for the lovely lass—something he had never allowed himself to face as squarely as he knew he should. He longed to share his thoughts with some good friend, but he was alone. Alone, that is, except for God; so again he raised his voice to heaven, surprising himself with an honest pronouncement.

"Dear Lord," he cried, *"I love her.* I have never admitted it, even to myself, but it is true. I love her. She, and you, dear God, are all that matter. Help me to live as she lives, to be worthy of her, and someday to woo her and win her for my own. . . ."

Samuel was weeping. Admitting his love for Susanna brought sudden release to seriously pent-up emotions—feelings too long enslaved in a prison of his own making—and the freedom he felt was overwhelming. He decided then to write her a letter at once.

Three times he composed a message before he was satisfied he had hidden the secret of his love. That he assumed he dare not divulge until some appropriate time in the far distant future. Such was the letter Susanna received and read again as she sat alone in the great house in Spital Yard, the day of the infamous execution.

A week later, when life in her father's house had returned to near normal, Susanna wrote to Sammy. And she, equally evasive, gave no hint of the love in her own heart. Samuel was glad to note that apparently there was no objection to his writing her; but, continuing to be cautious, he waited three weeks before answering her letter, and his second message was not unlike the first. Susanna, always prudent, waited an equal length of time to write; and the pattern of their correspondence was established for two long, uneventful years.

Because of Samuel's involvement in many activities at the university and the never-ending poverty that plagued him, his trips back to London were few and always brief. On those occasions, as a dutiful son, he spent most of his time with his mother. His Aunt Aggie had forgiven him for deserting the Dissenters, and, good woman that she was, made him as welcome and comfortable as she could.

Samuel had kept in close contact with John Dunton who, having married Elizabeth Annesley, was happy and doing well in the publishing business. Through a more spasmodic correspondence, Sam and Daniel Foe had kept in touch also, and the three friends always managed to meet at the coffee house near Newington Green. And, of course, Sammy never failed to make his way to the imposing brick structure in Spital Yard that continued to house the remnant of the Annesley clan. Only Judith, Anne, and Susanna remained beneath their father's roof. Their ailing mother was confined to her bed, and the pastor, who continued to serve the Little Saint Helens Church on Bishopsgate, was growing old.

Sammy and Sukey always found a place to sit and talk, thoroughly enjoying each other's company, while successfully concealing their innermost feelings. Strangely enough, neither of them guessed what the other was hiding.

Spring arrived early in southern England as Sammy was nearing the close of his third year at Oxford. The grass was turning green, the trees were in full bud, and a warm south wind brought smiles to the faces of old and young.

Sammy was especially happy. He had everything he needed. Others may have found that hard to believe, but it was being said that no one had ever given less to, and received more from the famous university than Samuel Wesley. He managed always to pay his bills, but poverty never ceased to stalk his steps. Even so, he was popular on campus. His threadbare coat and trousers were always neatly pressed and the frayed shirt he wore was fresh and clean.

As the warm sun smiled down upon the city, he could be seen jogging to and from classes, hurrying out to minister to convicts on death row, then back to his job of washing windows. Shortly before dark, he would go to his room where half a loaf of bread and some dried fruit awaited him. After thanking the Lord, he would eat, then turn to his books. His grades never fell below the upper level.

It was on just such an evening that a letter from his friend, John Dunton, arrived in the post. In it, John stated that he was contemplating publishing a periodical and that Danny Foe was deeply interested in it. He went on to say that Sam's cooperation was needed, and they were anxious that he meet with them, if possible, on April 12 at the coffee house in London. He and Danny were prepared to pay Sam's expenses.

So it happened that, on April 11, Samuel arrived in London and made his way to his mother's home.

The meeting at the coffee house the following day was interesting indeed. After the three friends had exchanged greetings and were seated, Dunton proceeded to enlighten Samuel with the projected plans for the enterprise.

"Our journal," he began, "will be different from anything Britain has ever seen. It will carry information which the people can receive from no other source." He went on to outline the ambitious plan.

The paper, to be called *The Athenian Gazette*, would be published twice each week, with the purpose of answering all questions that disturbed the reading public of the times. Dunton and Foe had enlisted the services of some of the most knowledgeable writers of the day, including Jonathan Swift, poet laureate Nahum Tate, Sir William Temple, and Sir Thomas Pope.

It is not difficult to believe that Sam Wesley's already healthy ego became greatly inflated when he found his name included in such a regal roster. His particular function, he was told, would be to answer all questions in the fields of divinity and ancient ecclesiastical history. And since he was adept at composing verse, the consensus was that if he were to frame his words of wisdom in rhyming couplets, the journal would be greatly enhanced. There was little doubt that he could rise to the occasion.

Sammy was sold. "Even if nothing ever were to come of the paper," he said, "what I have learned already from your plans makes this the greatest day of my life."

His statement was an obvious exaggeration, of course, and less than true in a sense of which he was totally unaware. The day held still greater things for Samuel.

Toward evening he made his way to Spital Yard. Spring was in the air. Birds whistling their mating calls, children laughing at their play, strangers smiling their pleasure as they met in the street, and finally, an elderly blind man, tapping his cane and humming a simple tune—all were equally responsible for the love that welled up in the heart of Sam Wesley as he approached the Annesley residence.

Sammy's resounding rap was answered by someone struggling with the bolt that secured the heavy door. Suddenly it opened and there, standing before the ambitious caller, was Susanna. Approaching seventeen, she was now possessed by the full bloom of womanhood. She seemed taller and more slender, as Sammy stood with eyes transfixed upon the most beautiful girl he had ever seen. Suddenly he longed—oh, how he longed—to take her in his arms, to caress her, to know that she was his forever. But no one would have guessed it, for this was the one—the only—area in which the extroverted Sammy was unbelievably shy.

A tiny hint of a smile, typical of Susanna, was his reward, and he treasured it. Then she quietly led him into the room where her sisters were standing by a small round table, deeply absorbed in viewing a canvas—a lovely painting spread before them. When they recognized the visitor, they came alive, greeting him with lavish smiles and words of warmest welcome. And he responded with his natural Irish wit and ease of manner that never failed to win him friends. Why, he wondered, could he not be equally at ease with Susanna? And she, poor girl, would have given anything—for a moment—to be like the vociferous Anne and Judith.

The sisters, seeming to sense the situation, excused themselves and hustled out to enjoy the warm spring afternoon, leaving the unconfessed lovers alone.

Samuel was strangely aware that he could no longer hide the secret that was burning in his heart. Susanna, already seated, invited him to take a chair; but instead he turned to face her squarely as he sought for appropriate words.

"Susanna," he began slowly, breaking the awful silence, "I have something to confess to you."

His cheeks felt hot; he knew he was blushing. "Bandying words around is supposed to be my forte," he said, "but right now I don't know how to say what's on my heart."

Susanna waited.

"Well, you see," he struggled on, "I'm twenty-three now, which means I have reached the age. . . . That is, I guess the time has come. . . . I know you will hate me for this, but I have secretly allowed myself to fall in love with you. What I'm trying to do is warn you that someday when I've finished my education and have been appointed to a living, I'll be asking you to marry me—to be my wife. I want you to have all the time you need to think about it."

He paused, and the ensuing silence filled him with despair. He hated himself as much as he loved the beautiful girl before him. Keeping the secret had been hurtful, but this was worse by a hundredfold.

Susanna, as usual, neither smiled nor frowned. No one could have guessed whether she were pleased or bored or disgusted.

"Samuel," she said, "I can give you my answer now."

"I see," he answered sadly. "I should have known. I've spoiled our beautiful friendship and you're disappointed and angry. The bad news is no less than I deserve. I will never forgive myself."

Her deep blue eyes penetrated the depths of his troubled soul.

"But I haven't told you whether the news is good or bad," she whispered.

He snapped to attention. "Do you mean. . . ?" he stammered.

"Yes, Sammy, I mean that I have loved you for a long, long time. I'll be proud to be your wife whenever the right time comes."

Samuel was overwhelmed. "I don't know what to say or do," he blurted.

Nothing moved but her lips.

"I think it would be perfectly proper," she said, "for you to take me in your arms and kiss me."

chapter 7
Just a Uniting

It was one of those rare, exciting days at Oxford. An important person was scheduled to give an address; and this time it was no less than James II, the King of England himself.

James, however, was not a popular monarch. Nearly every judgment he made was saturated with ulterior motives that only one more subtle than he would have succeeded in keeping under cover. Recently he had nominated a special friend for an important post at the school, who subsequently had failed to win the election. The king was angry as he approached the podium. Like a spoiled child, he hurled harsh, harassing threats upon his hearers in a most unkingly fashion.

Whatever bit of respect Samuel Wesley had held for His Royal Highness was turned to dust, as he witnessed the puerile performance. Sam kept well abreast of national and world affairs, and he never feared to speak or pen his strong convictions. This incident was not to be exempt from his comment.

Samuel graduated with a baccalaureate degree, and several months later was ordained a priest by the Bishop of Rochester. It was on that memorable day that James II, no longer able to endure the pressure of his office, abdicated the throne. William and Mary had already been declared sovereigns of Great Britain, and Samuel, in typical Wesley style, wrote and published the first pamphlet in support of the new administration. One of those little documents apparently found its way into the hands of the royal couple, for almost immediately, Sam received a naval chaplaincy at an excellent salary of seventy pounds a year.

Sam, upon receiving notice of his appointment, hurried to the house in Spital Yard. His heart was pounding as the now nineteen-year-old Susanna opened the door to greet him. Poor fellow, he could hardly contain his enthusiasm as he related the good news; and she, poor girl, was finding it equally hard to express the pride that filled her heart. Once again, she neither smiled nor frowned; and whether she was pleased or bored might have been anybody's guess.

"Sukey, dear," he said, "I will keep this job for just one short year. Then I'll ask the bishop for a curacy and eventually be appointed to a church. I've always wondered how I would be able to support you in the fashion you have enjoyed in your father's house. You have always been rich; I have always been poor. But now, with all my expenses paid plus seventy pounds, I finally feel free to ask you to marry me. At once, I mean. As soon as we can arrange a wedding. Please say you will."

Susanna remained silent for many moments; then, calmly meeting his dancing eyes, she framed her answer: "No, Sammy," she said, "since I will not be allowed to accompany you at sea. When we are married, I want to be your wife—to live with you, and work with you. Together we will rear our children—bring them up in the nurture and admonition of the Lord. We have waited a long time, dear. We can wait another year."

Lacey tethered his team to the hitching post in front of the coffee house near Newington Green. John Dunton had asked to meet him there. The little teamster was past sixty and his sandy hair had turned to snowy white, but he was as agile and sharp as ever. Inside the shop, he spied his friend at a half-secluded table near the back of the room.

"Sure and it's always nice to meet a friend," Lacey began the conversation. "I want you to know that I consider it a great honor to be asked to meet with so busy a man as you have come to be. It must be something important you have on your mind, so I'm hopin' I won't disappoint you."

"Have no fear of that, Lacey," Dunton answered. "I want to talk with you about our friends, Sam Wesley and the lovely Susanna. I've been married to Sukey's sister, Elizabeth, for a number of years, you know, and we are both deeply concerned for their welfare. Just before Sammy left for sea, they came to us to say they planned to marry as soon as he completed one full year in the chaplaincy.

"Lacey," Dunton continued, "you see, I'm talking about two of the best friends I have on earth. And Elizabeth has always felt responsible for her baby sister. We have strong reservations concerning their proposed matrimony. Ordinarily, of course, it would be none of our business; but in their case it is different. A marriage that doesn't work out will be a terrible disaster for such an extraordinary couple, and we fear it will kill Dr. Annesley. He has been a lonely man since his wife slipped away to heaven, and he has already endured more tragedies than most of us will ever know.

"You see, Lacey, Sammy and Sukey are so different in every way. Even their theology, which brought them together in the first place, is still a controversial issue with them. Neither Elizabeth nor I can see them making it as man and wife."

Lacey leaned forward to face his friend squarely. "And just why have you brought the problem to me?" he asked.

"Ah, my good fellow," John answered affectionately. "The whole Annesley family as well as many others have depended upon your good sense and counsel for years. Elizabeth and I are agreed that if anyone can help us with the touchy task that awaits us, you can. Tell me, how can we best go about it?"

"John," Lacey spoke seriously, "before we get to that, I want to ask you a question: What is your opinion—your honest appraisal—of Sam Wesley?"

The publisher answered without a hint of hesitation. "Sam is a great fellow," he said. "His heart is bigger even than his head; and that is quite a statement, for he is one of the most intelligent men I know. He has mastered Hebrew, Greek, and Latin. He is both an historian and a theologian of the first order; and he excels as a public speaker, especially in debate.

"And Sam is spiritually minded. He never fails in his ministrations to claim the inward witness of the Spirit as the proof of salvation. He should become one of the great preachers of the day."

"That's a strong recommendation, don't you know," Lacey suggested with a smile. "Now, is there anything to be said on the minus side?"

"Oh, yes, there is," Dunton answered quickly. "Sam is not conceited, but in some areas he holds an inflated opinion of his abilities. For instance, he's convinced that he's a poet, but I doubt that he will ever produce a poem of quality in all his life. He composes rhymes very well. I buy them from him all the time. He writes scholarly articles convincingly and well; but when he attempts a longer theme, he tends to bury his readers in heavy phrases and tedious details.

"I'm sure you must read what he writes in the *Gazette*. The depth of thought and wealth of knowledge he reveals through those clever couplets are outstanding. But he could do better. He writes too fast and far too much, if you understand what I am saying. We keep telling him that if he would compose half as many lines, spending twice the time on each one, his productions would border on perfection. If he could sense his limitations, he would ultimately enjoy much greater success. The problem is that he doesn't listen."

"I guess you are saying," Lacey interjected, "that genuine humility demands an accurate appraisal of one's self."

"Aye, will you say that again?" Dunton cried. "I must memorize it and write it down when I get back to my desk."

Lacey smiled. "Is that all?" he asked.

"No," John answered. "Sam has a tendency to be light and frivolous at times, even bordering on that which is absurd—if not actually repulsive. But he means no harm. He has a keen sense of humor which sometimes runs away with him."

"I think you have pictured Samuel very well," said Lacey. "Now, since I am not involved, family wise, as you and Elizabeth happen to be, let me tell you what I see when I look at Susanna and how it may relate to Sammy.

"I've been watching Sukey grow up since she was a three-year-old, reciting the Greek alphabet. I would guess that she has as great a mind as Samuel, but unlike him, she lacks the ability to display her feelings. If the dear girl has a sense of humor, she keeps it hidden; but even so she manages to be friendly and pleasant with everyone.

"It's true that, in her religion, she doesn't agree with the warm-hearted Samuel; but she lives better than he, for she keeps every Commandment to the letter. Her approach to the Almighty is intellectual, let us say. She has everything figured out, don't you know. She can't conceive of Samuel's inward witness that would give her the assurance of sins forgiven. Rather, she struggles daily to live without sinning.

"Samuel's approach to God is emotional—Dr. Annesley calls it experiential—and Sammy honors that warm relationship by living well—exceptionally well in areas he considers to be of prime importance. And even Sukey has to admit he enjoys his religion.

"Now, tell me, John, how have I done?"

"Excellent, Lacey, excellent. An accurate appraisal, I'm sure. But now to get back to our problem, how can we convince Sammy and Sukey that marriage for them would be a disaster?"

"Ah, my friend," Lacey responded. "We have finally reached the place where you and I are no longer in agreement. I hope that doesn't destroy the excellent fellowship we have always enjoyed; but since you admit you came today for advice and counsel, I'm going to take my stand.

"Samuel and Susanna are in love. It is not a

shallow infatuation, but a mutual affection of long standing. It goes deep. If that will not sustain them in the hard places, what in heaven's name will? There will be trying times, of course. What couple doesn't have them? But the fact that they are opposite in so many ways is in their favor. It will tend to keep them both in balance; they will learn from one another, and the years should bring them closer, don't you see?

"Now my advice is simply this: you and Elizabeth should go on living the good life you have chiseled out for yourselves. My faithful wife and I—and our son who is about to take over my not-too-lucrative business—will continue living ours. And none of us shall lift a finger to influence our precious friends. We will give them our congratulations and our blessings and our love.

"And if I don't miss my guess, we'll not be waiting until the end of the year to do it."

"What do you mean?" asked John, who was plainly swayed by the teamster's logic.

"I mean, it's going to be awfully lonesome for Sammy aboard that boat, with nothing but water to meet his gaze in any direction. And Sukey will be equally lonely in the mammoth house that no longer rings with the sounds of youth at their games and servants going about their duties. Only one maid is left and she comes for only a few hours each day. Susanna misses her mother more than anyone knows, and her father spends long hours in his study.

"Dr. Annesley's fortune, by the way, has dwindled to nearly nothing, mostly because of his liberal support of needy dissenting pastors for whom he feels grave responsibility. Susanna, who loves her father and shares his burdens, is probably near the end of her wits. She must long for Sammy.

"Methinks that the first time his vessel moves into the mouth of the Thames and wends its way to the city, Sammy will desert its dreary decks forever, and wedding bells will ring out from the tower of Little Saint Helens."

John Dunton studied his friend with admiration. "I believe you're right," he said.

"Do you, now?" Lacey smiled.

The little man's prophecy was good except for the ringing of the bells.

Dr. Annesley was sitting at his desk, deeply absorbed in an upcoming sermon, when he heard steps on the stair to his study. A moment later, Sukey and Sammy were facing him from the doorway.

"Well, now," he spoke kindly, pushing his books and papers aside. "Such sober faces as meet my gaze suggest that it's serious counsel you're seeking. Tell me, what is your problem?"

Susanna leveled her eyes upon her father. "Papa," she said, with neither a smile nor a frown, "Samuel and I wish to be married. We don't want even a little wedding; just a uniting here in your study this afternoon. We'll ask Judith and Anne to attend us.

"Sam has secured a curacy in London, and we

have rented rooms near Holborn. Mr. Lacey will be waiting with his rig to take us there as soon as we have exchanged our vows."

And that's the way it happened. Lacey reined up his well-groomed geldings in front of the tiny apartment. He bade the lovers the best of everything and leaned down to kiss the pretty bride on the forehead. Then he watched them as they entered their first home and closed the door behind them.

chapter **8**
The London Curacy

The newlyweds began their life together in the tiny, quaint apartment equipped with ancient, inexpensive furniture. The bare walls and glaring windows screamed for a woman's touch, which they were soon to receive at the hands of the meticulous Susanna. At the breakfast table that first morning, though, the lovers were surrounded with the stark reality of their plight; and Samuel lacked the imagination to visualize the transformation that would come.

"I'm sorry, Sukey," he said. "This must be a terrible shock to you after living in the lovely home your father provided for his family. I wish I had something better to offer you."

"Pish," she answered without either smile or frown, while an unmistakable warmth radiated from the beautiful countenance Sammy faced across the table. *How he loved her!*

"When I bring my things," she said, "my

paintings, my rugs and dishes, and everything else, you will think we have moved to a better part of the city. You'll see." She gazed steadily into his adoring eyes. *How she loved him!*

"As soon as I get back to my writing, I will be able to supplement our meager salary," he promised. "Someday when I have been appointed to a church of my own, the Lord will supply all our needs." His expressive countenance glowed with pleasure.

Susanna studied her husband carefully. She knew he was a dreamer who found it easy to live in pleasant anticipation of better days ahead. If there was anything cold about the young bride, it was her practicality, for she lived in neither the yesterdays nor the tomorrows.

"Samuel," she stated firmly, "your optimism is heartening, but heaven will help us only when we are doing everything we can to solve our problems ourselves. The Lord will give us a family to rear for his glory; he will use our lives if we keep his Commandments, and that will be more than we deserve. Right now, we must faithfully serve the curacy you have been given."

"Yes, dear," he answered. Then, smiling broadly, but speaking seriously nonetheless, he continued, "God has given me just the wife and companion I need to assist me. That I see clearly."

The curates were assistant pastors, hired by the rectors, or ministers in charge. These young men were important, for without them there would have been hardly a pastor available for the people in the thousands of smaller churches across Great Britain. Usually, they were poorly paid by their superiors.

The higher offices in the established church and the better livings were often for sale, and the salaries—provided through universal taxation—were large. It was not uncommon for a rector to hold as many as four appointments, each providing a good income out of which he paid a mere pittance to the curates who carried the burdens of the churches under his charge. Too often, those rectors had little or no interest in the spiritual welfare of the people—nor in their own—and they spent their days in secular pursuits and worldly pleasures. So it was not unusual for the curates to reflect the godlessness of their superiors and, in so doing, assure their own security as they waited for better appointments.

It was to such a curacy that Samuel Wesley had been appointed at thirty pounds per annum, which was considerably less than half the salary he had received from his naval chaplaincy.

The rector under whom Samuel was to labor probably expected apathy and infidelity in his new assistant, but only because he did not know his man. Both Samuel and Susanna were aware of the low spiritual level and undisciplined behavior of the people, and they were determined to effect radical changes in the church they served.

The first Sunday morning, Susanna took her place near the front of the sanctuary and watched with pride as her husband gracefully, solemnly took his place at the lectern. There was something about him that demanded the attention and respect of everyone. No bishop could have read the Scriptures and prayers with greater dignity and grace, and none could have entered the high pulpit with more awesome authority than her beloved Samuel.

Sam had chosen unpopular, controversial issues for his first discourse. Hardly a minister could have been found who was capable of presenting such sound logic and irrefutable arguments.

He preached with power. The people were clearly impressed, surprised that so capable a minister had come to so small a church. But in the congregation there were wealthy, worldly men and their aristocratic spouses who feared and resented the strong voice that dared to invade their private lives and expose their sins. And it was they, of course, who controlled the purse strings and wielded power in high places. But there were also honest, hungry souls who listened, yearning for the truth they hadn't heard for a long time, and they blessed the one who dared to preach it with no apparent fear of the consequences.

So, at that initial service, factions were already forming and trouble lurked in the shadows. Samuel, however, was too naive on the one hand,

and too determined on the other, to sense it; and he was too hard-headed to care when he found it to be true.

Susanna was aware of the problem from the outset, and it was she, with rare diplomacy, who delivered the message to her husband.

"That's the way it is, Sammy," she said. "I remember my father facing the same situation."

"Do you mean I should compromise the plain word of the Scriptures to please the carnal tastes of a bunch of hypocrites?" he demanded. Never had he spoken so sharply to Susanna since the days of their early discussions. She may have been hurt, but she kept it hidden. He was sorry, and it showed.

"It's all right, Samuel," she said. "I'm on your side—remember? I only want you to recognize the enemy when you go into battle. Please don't make the mistake, now, of shooting from ambush. Be sure of the truth you represent, and preach it. You may feel sometimes that you're losing the skirmish—but you will win the war."

He thanked her fervently. "What would I do without you?" he asked honestly. Then, together, they knelt by their chairs and prayed for strength and wisdom, grace and love—and victory.

The breach in the congregation widened, but the people continued to attend the services in growing numbers. Even the opposition increased numerically as Sammy's sermons were scrutinized and dissected in a constant search for heresy or other damaging evidence upon which to demand his release.

At the same time, there were honest hearts who, convicted of their sins, sought the pastor's counsel in search of the inward witness he claimed was the will and the gift of God. But while Samuel was adept at presenting the need for repentance, he never acquired a talent for "drawing the net."

Ironically, it was in regard to the inward witness that Susanna had never come into agreement with Sammy's theology. *But,* he argued with himself, *she lives so well, I will never make it an issue again. I'll leave it with the Lord.*

The first five weeks of married life passed quickly as Susanna transformed the drab apartment into a place of peace and pleasure. The ugly chairs were hidden beneath colorful covers of material she had brought from Spital Yard, and the rough table upon which they ate their meager meals became a board of beauty with its linen cloth and silver centerpiece. Pictures on the walls; rugs on the floors; books on the shelves— a place for everything and everything in its place—all this and more was hard for Sammy to believe. And there was something else to astound him that demanded his unwilling cooperation. For the first time in his life, he found himself involved in a disciplined household. An hour to retire, an hour to rise; a time for meals, a time for prayers; everything carefully rationed, even the food that was set before him.

When Samuel complained a bit about the latter, Susanna faced him squarely. "If I give you more today," she said, "you'll be *forced* to fast on Friday."

He thanked her, noting that the portions she allowed herself were half the size of the ones she set before him.

It was then that he began to sense a terseness in her manner, a sort of "needling" in her voice when he failed to conform to the pattern she had established for their home. It was no new development in the young bride's personality; Elizabeth had detected it when Sukey was only eleven years old. Alarmed by it, she had told her father, "I sense a certain sting in her words when she's displeased, a crispness that seems to say, 'Watch your step or I will put you in your place.'"

Whatever it was, it conveyed an early message to Samuel that there were levels at which Susanna would always claim control. He yielded quietly, for he could see that the authority she assumed was limited to the areas of her special responsibility. Beyond that, while she might not have fully agreed, she calmly resigned herself to the Apostle Paul's admonition to "be subject to her husband in all things." Without question, Samuel Wesley had chosen a most extraordinary lady to share his life, and already he was learning important lessons from her.

Immediately after breakfast, they read from the Scriptures and knelt together in solemn, earnest prayer. Following devotions, Susanna dusted and polished the tiny apartment, after which she spent two full hours alone in meditation and study. Then she went into her little kitchen to prepare the noonday meal, which Sammy soon discovered would be served at the stroke of twelve.

So he adopted a pattern of his own. Three hours on Monday and Tuesday mornings were spent in writing articles and couplets for *The Athenian Gazette*. Those same hours, the next two days, he gave to sermon preparation. Friday mornings were devoted to the writing of "heavy" poetry, but those projects failed to sell.

Samuel spent the afternoon hours among the people. He was an incessant and effective caller as he visited with needy souls who were oppressed by the trying times. His Irish wit and optimism provided just the stimulant they needed. It can be said that Sam was a "people person" and a man's man. Even those worldly fellows in his church who sought his dismissal couldn't help but like him. It was his fearless preaching they resented.

Matrons in the congregation sought his kindly counsel in their efforts to serve the Lord and rear their families in the faith. It was an awful era of great challenge. Great numbers of unwed girls were forced into prostitution, as they had no other means of support. It was not unusual for two or three of these unfortunate young women to slip quietly into the worship service, probably to escape the elements. It was they who needed understanding and direction, but Samuel was unable to face their plight with any degree of objectivity, and they sensed it.

But there was something about the lovely sober countenance of the unsmiling, unfrowning Susanna that provoked their faith and trust. How can one explain it? How can a woman whose virtue has never been questioned, whose life has been blissfully sheltered—one who has kept the Commandments consistently from childhood—comprehend the plight of girls "of the street"?

There seems to be no answer; but more than once, just such a fallen lass would knock in desperation at the door of the little apartment. She was there to pour out her heart and confess her sins to the nineteen-year-old bride of the youthful curate, whom she was sure would hear her story and pray for her soul.

Susanna had no formula for recovery, no words of wisdom to offer her despondent guest—she was neither a social worker nor a missionary in any professional sense—but she listened well. Her strength was in her virtue, her compassion, her love—gifts that spoke louder than sermons. Her witness was a glistening tear, a loving pat on the hand, and a fleeting kiss on the cheek as the repenting soul departed. The record is kept in heaven.

Samuel was unaware of the quiet, unpretentious ministry Sukey was performing, for she kept it a secret. Her husband, so bound by tradition, would not have granted his approval, she was certain of that. Convention was strong and she was guilty of two violations: ministry was for men, and households of the decent were not to be defiled by the presence of harlots. But she couldn't blame Sammy. He didn't make the rules; he kept them.

Friday night ended the work week for the Wesleys. Saturday was different. Sam and Susanna relaxed from their arduous schedule and could spend the day together, mostly strolling the streets of the city. They visited the new St. Paul's Cathedral, which, under the direction of Sir Christopher Wren, was slowly becoming an architectural masterpiece. For centuries it would dominate the metropolis. Together they knelt to pray in beautiful St. Giles where Susanna's father had been pastor of the city's largest congregation. Hand in hand, they strolled the grassy banks of the Thames and wandered on to the palace of all the kings and queens of England since William the Conqueror. These were the happiest days of their lives. Especially so, since Susanna had announced to an ecstatic Sammy that their firstborn was on the way.

The winter of 1689-90 was unusually pleasant. There were some dreary days, of course, but crisp, sunshiny weather dominated the scene. London's streets and shops were alive with happy, smiling faces; even the congregation, seriously divided, was unusually congenial. Sammy, naturally good-natured, was certain his troubles were over; but Susanna, aware of his naivete, continued to be cautious.

"Be sure of what you believe, and preach it," she advised him. "But don't expect Satan to say amen."

In February the baby came, and to the delight of both the parents, it was a boy. What did Susanna name him? Well, with a father and a brother and a husband all bearing the name of Samuel, what would one expect?

The first Sunday in June developed into one of those rare days everyone talks about. Baby Samuel was nearly four months old, and Susanna carried him proudly to the church where, as always, they were the center of attraction.

"Madonna and child," a woman whispered as they entered the sanctuary; and, surely, one might wonder where an artist could find more excellent models for that ancient theme. Even Conrad Sager, a man of means and leader of the militant minority that planned to unseat her Sammy, gave the pretty mother and her babe a patronizing smile.

Susanna, however, was not easily flattered, and she saw at a glance that the opposing forces were present en masse that morning.

Then, just as the service was getting underway, the minister in charge, or rector, who had never heard Samuel preach, made his appearance accompanied by a man of unmistakable elegance—an important person to be sure.

From the lectern, Samuel surveyed the situation and glanced at Susanna, who flashed a rare and fleeting smile in positive response. It conveyed a dozen messages in one, including, "I love you, Sammy. . . don't worry, dear, God is still on the throne," and certainly it suggested that he preach with all the powers of persuasion he possessed. It was just the tonic he needed.

Samuel was at his best. The dignity and poise with which he conducted the service approached perfection. It was all so commendable that deep concern registered on the faces of those who opposed him. How could anyone demand the removal of so excellent a minister? They waited impatiently for the sermon, hoping, of course, that as usual it would be so offensive to the wealthy that their request for a change would be honored without question. They were certain that the rector was on their side—for, not only was he a man of questionable morals himself, but he could hardly afford to face their displeasure. They were fully aware, though, that two-thirds of the congregation were in love with the Wesleys and willing to abide the preaching. Would the powers that be dare override so great a majority? And who, they asked themselves, was the dignified stranger accompanying the rector? That was also an unanswered question in the minds of Samuel and Susanna.

But Sammy, as he mounted the stair to the pulpit, cared not whom or what the stranger was, nor why the rector came to church, nor what the opposition planned to do. He knew that he was standing in the center of the will of the omnipotent, omnipresent God, for a peace beyond understanding enveloped his soul. The inexplicable warmth of the inward witness was aglow within his breast. As he opened the mammoth Bible before him, he knew that his beloved wife—holding their precious son—was calmly petitioning the Throne of Grace in his behalf. Nothing else mattered.

He read from the eighth chapter of Job (his favorite Old Testament character), pinpointing verse thirteen as his text: "So are the paths of all that forget God; and the hypocrite's hope shall perish."

In context he quoted Jesus' warnings to the scribes and Pharisees, followed by his words of instruction to his friends: "Verily I say unto you, Except ye be converted, and become as little children, ye shall not enter into the kingdom of heaven" (Matt. 18:3).

Samuel may never have preached again with equal power and passion. He quoted nothing but the Word, and while he was adept at editorializing, this day he drew no personal conclusions and made no specific applications of the truths he expounded. And that was well, for he could only have dulled the "two-edged sword," which indeed he knew can prick the conscience and sever a soul from Satan's grasp.

Later, Susanna described the service to her father. "The very atmosphere," she said, "was charged with the awful presence of God. Following the benediction, the people were loath to leave.

"Samuel came down to the people and the rector arose to introduce the stranger at his side. It was none other than John Sheffield, the Marquis of Normanby.

"The good man held Samuel's hand in his own and thanked him for the message. 'I am a sinful man,' he said, 'who, like thousands of others, plans to do better later along. I make no pretense of living a life that is pleasing to heaven, but I know and appreciate truth when I hear it. Would that every minister in the city this morning were as honest and fearless as you have been.'

"In the light of his honest confession and kindly spoken words," she concluded, "none dared to raise a voice in opposition to Sammy."

For several weeks, the services continued with no outward display of hostility, but the ambitious Samuel was showing signs of boredom. At least, that was Susanna's diagnosis of a restlessness that overtook him, and nothing she could say or do would dispel it.

Then, in mid-July, Samuel received a letter from South Ormsby, a small town that, in those days, was considered to be a long way north of London. It was signed, "The Massingberds." It stated simply that the rector of their church had died and Samuel had been highly recommended to succeed him by the Marquis of Normanby, who had heard him preach in London. The Marquis spent much of his time there at his country seat. The letter went on to say that steps necessary to Samuel's appointment would be cared for expeditiously if he should accept the call. The living was small, it said—just fifty pounds per annum; and the rectory, old and unpretentious, was as good or slightly better than the average dwelling in the village. A brief postscript read, "The work is not too demanding, which will leave ample time for you to pursue your avocation. We understand that you are a gifted writer."

Sammy and Sukey were elated, and they thanked the Lord that they might rear their family in a rural setting, far from the wicked metropolis.

They straightway accepted the invitation. In August, they moved to South Ormsby.

chapter 9

South Ormsby

Susanna, holding baby Samuel, stood studying the drab little house of reeds and clay that was to be the Wesleys' home for whatever years they would spend in South Ormsby. To the back, on higher ground, stood the ancient church of St. Leonard. Poor as it all appeared to be, Susanna felt a flush of pride, for it represented her husband's first real pastoral appointment. She was anxious to inspect the inside of the tiny rectory; but she had to wait, for Samuel had gone for the key. When he returned, the family of three entered the unpretentious dwelling together.

"I was hoping it would be better than this," Samuel observed with a tinge of embarrassment. "It seems that all I do is disappoint you."

"I'll fix it up, Sammy, you know that," she answered. "We'll be warm and cozy through the winter. Just be sure you get in plenty of fuel.

Next spring we'll plant grass and flowers, and if you will paint those awful shutters we'll have the neatest home on the street. And that will honor God."

The village people appeared to be embarrassed at the advent of the new rector and his family and were slow to extend a welcome. The Wesleys, in turn, felt strange and unwanted, which was especially hard for the congenial Sammy to accept. Neither he nor Sukey had known anything other than city life, so naturally the mixing of the cultures was going to take time and effort on the part of all.

Samuel, trying too hard to win the people, put them on their guard. So it was the reserved, unsmiling Susanna who first won her way into their hearts. Later, one the nicest ladies in the church admitted that she had wanted to bring in food for the family the day of their arrival, but she was "afraid city folks wouldn't like country cooking."

Sunday, of course, was the day of the first real test. If Samuel had exuded even a hint of looseness or levity in the worship that morning, it might have delayed his acceptance by months or years. But there was no danger of his being guilty of such impropriety. To him, the church was a divine institution; its liturgy sacred; and his personal obligation to God and the people an awesome responsibility.

Susanna beamed with pride and pleasure as he opened the service. She was reminded of a compliment paid him by Lacey, who, after visiting their church in Holburn, had said, "Sure and the angel Gabriel himself could hardly have done it better."

The people were surprised and pleased beyond measure. Their former rector had been "easy" in his ministrations. He had been clumsy in the liturgy and faltering in the pulpit. One of the laymen described his sermons as "gummers," a term he and his fellow farmers used to describe aging sheep that had lost their teeth. So the change was startling, to say the least.

It was good, if not providential, that Samuel's performance pleased the people. Otherwise, the unvarnished truth he preached might not have been accepted. If some of the people were offended, they kept it under cover. After all, these were gentle country folk who knew the standards of good behavior. As a result of that initial sermon, many of them resolved to take inventory of their lives, and they proceeded to do better. Samuel was off to an excellent start.

No less responsible for an upward moral trend in the parish, however, was the carefully disciplined life and kindly spirit of the inimitable Susanna. The people knew exactly where she stood. "Any time in the afternoon or evening," she told them, "the rectory is open for counsel and instruction. But only in emergency should the rector or myself be disturbed in the morning hours. Our family prayers, Samuel's study and writing, and my own time of private devotions must be carefully observed."

Not only did they respect her wishes, but it

was said that some of them established "family altars" of their own.

The winter of 1690-91 was unusually cold and wet. The drafty house needed more repairs than Samuel had realized; but a blazing fire in the hearth, together with heavy quilts provided by the people, kept the little family from suffering. Susanna's strength, however, was waning. Her arduous schedule, the care of baby Sam, and the fact that a second child was expected in the spring, were taking their toll. By January, she was forced to spend much of her time in bed. Samuel was kind and tried to be helpful; but he, poor man, was as awkward in the home as he was graceful in the church. Yet he did his best.

A baby girl whom they named Susanna arrived much earlier than expected. She was tiny and weak and seldom cried as she lay listlessly on her little bed, taking no turn for the better. Then, one chilly, windy morning when even the fire refused to burn beneath the drafty chimney, and beads of sleet began to batter the rattling windows, Susanna bravely faced her despairing husband.

"This one," she said sadly, "we will soon be giving back to God. He will give us more; and some of them, he will let us keep. The fortunate ones will be those he takes, for they will be safe in heaven. The others will live to bless our lives, but they will know what it means to suffer. It will be our responsibility to see that they serve the Lord, and he will use them."

Samuel wept. He took the tiny child in his arms and held her to his breast. "Sukey," he said softly, "you never cease to amaze me. What you just said was a new thought to me. I know you're right, but I will never willingly release one of these little ones, even when I know it's to heaven."

"Of course you won't, Sammy," she answered. "We will cry over every one of them, but God will comfort our hearts and wipe away our tears. We must never fail, even for a moment, to be thankful in all things, for this is his will."

"Sukey," Samuel responded thoughtfully, "I've always known why God willed that we spend our lives together. I need you. You are strong—so strong—where I am weak. I don't know what I would do without you."

Five days later the baby died, but another little girl was born the following year to take her place. They named her Emilia and called her Emily. She was a lively, robust child who brought love, warmth, and sunshine into the little rectory even in the darkest of days. And the bright-eyed two-and-a-half-year-old Sammy, Jr., with never a jealous moment, loved her. The two were best of friends from the outset.

The summer of 1692 came early. Susanna regained her strength, but the vitality of her youth was plainly fading. Never again would she be seen as the pretty bride of the pastor, but as a mature and lovely matron, weighted with responsibilities. She continued to practice her disciplined life as the paradox of her pleasant, unsmiling personality became more and more evident to all who knew her. The fun-loving Samuel longed in vain to hear her laugh along with their friends at his Irish humor, but it didn't matter. He loved her dearly. Nothing could change that.

The first four years at South Ormsby were profitable ones for the Wesleys. Their home, while barely adequate for their needs, made it possible for them to live with a minimum of expense; and the fifty-pounds-per-annum salary was supplemented by at least that much more through Samuel's writing—mostly for *The Athenian Gazette*. The months melted into years.

In 1694, twins were born, but neither of them lived through the winter. It was not an easy time for Susanna physically, she was weak, and added to her burdens was a deep concern for Sammy, Jr. At four years of age, he had made no attempt to talk. The lad was bright, always cognizant of what was going on around him; he cried when his father told him God was taking the twins to heaven, but no word—not even Mama—ever escaped his lips.

Samuel was more deeply disturbed than Susanna—especially since tiny Emily, not yet three, was putting words together to make sentences.

Sammy, Jr., loved his sister, and while he paid little attention to what grownups were saying, he listened carefully to every word the little one uttered. Susanna's faith took hold when she caught her son whispering to himself. She was certain he was experimenting with lips and tongue, quietly practicing the words his sister was glibly spewing. It seemed he had inherited the perfectionism of his mother. He would speak no word until he could do it exactly right.

Then came an afternoon when both Sammy, Jr., and his pet cat disappeared. Neighbors and friends were alerted. They hurried out in all directions, as every house, every barn, every ditch, even the trees were searched to no avail.

Samuel was nearly beside himself; but Susanna, with characteristic calmness, held tiny Emily by the hand as she combed the area in, around, and under the little rectory. She peered into the attic, then went back to her kitchen. The table upon which the family ate their meals was covered with a large checkered cloth which nearly reached the floor. No one had bothered to look beneath it, nor did Susanna as she stood less than three feet away, staring through a window to the meadow beyond.

Then, almost in desperation, she called sternly, *"Samuel, Junior,* where are you?"

From under the table came the reply. "Here I am, Mother."

The search was ended; so was the consternation regarding Sammy's failure to talk. The problem thereafter, so Samuel, Sr., said, was finding ways to keep him quiet.

In 1695 another girl was born. Samuel insisted upon calling her Susanna, since the first one

named for her mother had died. This second
Susanna was a healthy child, as was yet another
born the following year. She was christened
Mary.

By 1695 serious troubles had begun to harass
the rector of South Ormsby. First, there was a
problem of conscience. He had failed to see the
revival for which he continued to pray with fervor. His preaching convicted the people of their
sins, but no one, not even his beloved Susanna,
had received that inward witness for which he
contended strongly. Samuel blamed himself—
rightly so, perhaps—for his quick temper and
sharp criticism often tended to unravel the fabric
of his most earnest endeavors.

Then there came a breach in Samuel's relationship with John Dunton. While that may not
have been the reason the eccentric publisher decided to discontinue *The Athenian Gazette*, the
journal did indeed draw one last fleeting breath,
leaving Samuel without the income upon which
he had so strongly depended.

At about this same time, Susanna was in
mourning over the death of her sister Elizabeth,
whose life with Dunton had been a happy one.
John married again in less than half a year, and
this in turn probably hastened a break with the
Wesleys.

Then Dr. Annesley died, bringing deep sorrow to both Susanna and Samuel, although the
sad news didn't reach them for several weeks.
Also, in the midst of their mourning, baby Mary

sustained a serious fall which nearly took her life. The accident left her weak and somewhat deformed in body, adding greatly to the family's burdens.

If Samuel had not believed that God was preparing the way for a great spiritual awakening— one which he began to sense he probably wouldn't live to witness—he might have broken beneath the strain. Susanna was much stronger than her husband throughout those weeks of trial and testing.

It is no wonder that Samuel, who by then must have found it easy to identify with his favorite Old Testament character, Job, decided to do a series of dissertations on the patient man of God. But the end was not yet, for as in the case of the ancient patriarch, greater troubles came to harass him. The next one involved a situation that was to destroy the good relationship Samuel had managed to maintain with the church and community.

In a town of three hundred residents, secrets are hard to keep and rumors roll. One story was that a certain pretty widow called Lutie was the mistress of the Marquis of Normanby. The rumor was strengthened by the fact that the Marquis's wife seldom accompanied him to his country place known as the Hall at South Ormsby. The Wesleys, however, were supposed to be protected from hearing such rumors, for it was deemed improper to report anything of such a derogatory nature to the preacher. So it was a bit ironic that the rectory was the only house in town wherein the real truth of the matter was known.

It happened that one afternoon while Samuel was visiting among the people, Lutie called upon Susanna. The gracious hostess guessed the woman's problem, for she reminded her of the girls of the street who had come to her door in Holburn. The troubled guest was given the best chair in the house, and Susanna's kindly, sober countenance drew forth from her an honest, full confession of her sins.

The counselor's only comment was, "Mind the Lord, my dear. I will include you in my prayers. Come again whenever you like, but be sure to choose a time when I'm alone." Then, with a pat on the hand and a soft kiss on the cheek, she went with her to the door.

The following week the Marquis, having returned to town, immediately made arrangements for Samuel to visit him. Sam spent most of an afternoon at the Hall, in earnest consultation with his friend; and no one, not even Susanna, was ever enlightened regarding the reason for their discussion. Keeping the counsel of others is a sacred responsibility, one that never was violated by either Samuel or Susanna.

From the early days of history, illicit sex has been deemed a greater sin in women than in men—but not in the clear-thinking mind of Susanna. There was little, however, that she could do to correct this prejudice. Samuel took its reality for granted. He was prepared to pray for male offenders, making them welcome anywhere; but unconsciously, he entertained little hope for a fallen woman, and certainly he would never consent to one entering (defiling) the sanctity of his home.

This disagreement was the basis for an unfortunate scene when, on a later occasion, Samuel returned unexpectedly home to find Lutie and Susanna engaged in serious conversation. Sammy's Irish ire flared and, without a word, he took the "offensive creature" by the hand, escorted her unceremoniously out of the house, and slammed the door. This unfortunate incident triggered the first of many family fights between the Wesleys; but it didn't destroy their love.

Another problem emerged, however, for nosy neighbors saw Lutie being expelled from the rectory and heard something of the fracas that followed. This, naturally, made life well-nigh unbearable for both Samuel and Susanna. And there was no end to speculation when later the rector announced that he had been offered and was accepting an appointment to Epworth, a town of two thousand inhabitants with a much larger church, across the county from South Ormsby. The consensus was that the Marquis had arranged to have his friend transferred to greener pastures.

Actually, it was through the nobleman's earlier efforts in Samuel's behalf that the way was opened for the present promotion. For a long time the Marquis had tried to persuade the crown to appoint Samuel to the bishopric of Ireland. "The position is open," he had argued, "and Mr. Wesley has all the qualifications; training [he had acquired a master's degree by then], leadership, talent, grace; even enough Irish blood and the characteristics that accompany it, to render him wholly acceptable to the churches in the Emerald Isle."

It was a strong nomination, to be sure, even though it was rejected in favor of an older man who had long been under consideration for the post. It is believed, however, that shortly before Queen Mary died, she had made known her wish that Mr. Wesley be awarded a better living at Epworth. And if ever a family needed a better living it was the Wesleys in that desperate hour.

Samuel borrowed 150 pounds to clear the debts he had accumulated after losing his income from *The Athenian Gazette,** and to purchase a team of horses with which to make the move. Since the new living was to pay him 200 pounds per annum—four times as much as he had ever received before—he saw no reason to worry. Susanna, however, tended to be skeptical. She had come to know her impractical husband well enough to doubt that any degree of wealth would ever be theirs. Both she and Samuel were happy, though, as they packed their possessions into a cumbersome, four-wheeled wagon to begin their journey across the spongy, wet trails of rural Lincolnshire.

*The name had been changed to *The Athenian Mercury*.

chapter **10**
"Revival Will Come"

After the longest, roughest, most tiresome ride imaginable, Samuel sighted the town of Epworth. Susanna and the four children were sound asleep, so tired that nothing, it seemed, could rouse them. What Sammy saw was a dreary place with muddy streets winding between thatched clay dwellings, and a scattering of brick and stone buildings that he guessed were houses of commerce. The most impressive structure to meet his gaze was the ancient church of St. Andrews to which he had been appointed rector.

It was late in the afternoon. Samuel stopped the team and Susanna awoke immediately, the sudden change of pace being more startling to her weary body than all the bumpy terrain they had traversed.

"There's our town," Sammy announced. "The sun is to our left, so we are facing north. We want to have our directions right. You can see the church. It is larger and better than I expected."

"Where is the rectory?" asked Susanna.

"I understand it is only a piece from the chapel," he answered. "We'll be there soon. I am told there is a barn, so I will feed and bed down the horses while you fix some victuals and improvise some cots. The Lord knows we all need a good night's rest."

A few moments later, they pulled up to a three-story parish house built with timbers and plaster and covered with thatch. At least it was much more commodious and of better construction than the tiny house in South Ormsby, but it was old and not in the best repair. The barn was worse. Around the rectory was the glebe—several acres that belonged to the church, to be used by the rector.

Hardly had the Wesleys alighted from their wagon when a pretty, outgoing matron of middle age and her gangly, bashful husband, dressed for the fields, hurried over to welcome the new parsonage family. The extroverted lady introduced herself and her husband as Cora and Calvin O'Conner.

"Sounds Irish, doesn't it," she said, flashing a contagious smile. "We're really Scotch," she explained. "Calvin was an adopted boy. That's how he got the name O'Conner."

Susanna acknowledged the introduction pleasantly enough with neither smile nor frown, as Sammy tried to say something to the effect that they were happy to be met by so congenial a couple; but the talkative Cora rattled on.

"We must help you get the wagon unloaded. There's lightning in that bank of black clouds moving in. It may be raining by nightfall, and when it rains, *it rains*, especially this time of year.

"Calvin, gather up some kindling and get a fire going in the hearth. The house has been empty for quite awhile. It's bound to be clammy and cold inside," she continued.

"As soon as we have your things under cover, I'll run home and fetch a pot of tea. You must be terribly tired.

"Calvin, as soon as you get that fire started, pitch down some hay for the horses, and show the rector the barn.

"Oh, Mrs. Wesley—that is your name, isn't it— what lovely children. It will be so nice to hear them at their play. It's been a long time since the rectory rang with the sound of babies. I do hope you'll like it here." There seemed to be no end to her chatter. "I'll help you get acquainted. The people are not easy to get on with, as you will soon discover, but just be yourselves and take your stand."

Samuel and Susanna were astonished and amused at Cora's incessant flow of information and instruction; but wisely, they didn't allow it to show. And Sammy was pleased that Calvin, as soon as he was away from his vociferous spouse, was warm and friendly, and extremely knowledgeable in his own right.

As soon as the welcoming committee had gone

home, Samuel remarked that if all the people of Epworth were as congenial as the O'Conners, loneliness should be no problem.

"I have a feeling." Susanna answered thoughtfully, "we won't find many people here like Cora and Calvin. I think they were trying to compensate for a cold, unfriendly welcome we'll be experiencing later."

The Wesleys, even Sammy, Jr., and Emily, sighed their relief to be alone with a fire crackling on the hearth and clean white beds ready to receive their aching bodies. Susanna had never seen Samuel so worn and weary; and she, heavy with child, was at the end of her endurance. As she tucked the little ones into their beds, a flash of lightning, followed by a rolling peal of thunder, shook the walls and rattled the windows, announcing the arrival of a warm spring downpour. They crawled gratefully between the covers, and long into the night, a steady rain beat against the building like a lullaby from heaven. The family slept the dreamless sleep of pilgrims, weary from the road, but possessed of a calm assurance that they were serving a living, loving Father to the fullness of their strength.

Samuel and Susanna awakened shortly after dawn. The children were still sleeping soundly, so they quietly dressed and went out to view their new surroundings. The storm had passed in the night, leaving the morning air wonderfully fresh and invigorating. First the couple made their way to the church and stood amazed and delighted with the quaint, lovely sanctuary. The center area of the massive structure dated back five hundred years, to the time of the Crusades. The original building, having deteriorated badly through the ages, had undergone remodeling a quarter-century before, which was a fortunate turn in its history.

Next they walked across the spongy glebe with water filling in their tracks behind them. Enjoying clean, clear atmosphere, strong with the scent of springtime and alive with sounds of bleating sheep and birdsong, was not unlike entering a pleasant dream. Every tiny blade that had pushed its way up through the soil encouraged the happy newcomers. Life was here. They loved it, and they loved each other. For that wonderful hour together, they were supremely happy.

By the end of the week, Susanna had arranged to best advantage every bit of furniture she could call her own. Much more was needed to turn the large old house into a comfortable home, which meant, of course, that another loan would have to be secured. She talked it over with Samuel, who had no worries. The promised 200 pounds per annum, plus the money from the sale of "poems" he planned to write, seemed like a fortune to the optimistic young man.

"Not only will we have furniture," he assured her, "but there will be servants to do the work. Caring for the children and listening to my troubles will take all your time and strength. Remember, now, I always said that someday I would provide for you as your father did before I took you away from Spital Yard."

Susanna didn't readily respond. She had serious doubts that all his hopes would materialize; but she wasn't lacking in appreciation, for she knew he was sincere.

Finally she said, "I know you mean well, Sammy. You would like to do all that and more."

Sunday morning dawned bright and clear and the people poured into church—particularly, of course, to assess their new shepherd and get a close view of his family.

Samuel and Susanna, immaculate in dress and demeanor, faced the exciting prospect of a first worship service in the impressive sanctuary of St. Andrews. They were glad for the experiences they had gained at South Ormsby. They assumed, of course, that they had become fully acquainted with the ways of country people and that "fitting in" would no longer pose a problem. Actually, except for the O'Conners and several families who operated the stores and offices in town, there was hardly a soul in the whole community who could read and write.

Susanna, as always, took her place in the church. Her children, sparkling clean and carefully dressed, were sitting straight as little soldiers beside her, for she wanted so much to make a good impression. It wasn't long, though, before serious doubts began to assail her. Less than half the people resembled the gentle rural folk of South Ormsby. Many of the men were dressed in the same clothes they wore in the fields all week, for they had no Sunday suits. Their women, with deep, tanned faces and scraggly hair, herded their unkempt youngsters into the pews, and no one smiled a welcome or even appeared to notice the rector's pretty family.

Then, just as Samuel was about to open the service, a dozen or more rough young men marched down the center aisle and were seated. Their grim faces bespoke the hatred in their hearts, and Susanna was certain they were there for no good purpose.

Nervously she watched and listened to Samuel, who expressed no awe and minced no words as he performed his ministrations. At the close of the service, the people leaving the church were as cold and noncommittal as when they had entered.

Only the O'Conners and several of their friends waited to greet the Wesleys, to assure them they were headed squarely down the only road that would lead to victory.

That first Sunday afternoon, a visitor came to the rectory. Samuel opened the door and looked up into the sober face of Calvin O'Conner. He had come alone.

"I would like to talk with you and your good wife," he said. "If you have any questions, I will try to answer them."

"Yes, Calvin, come in, come in," Samuel responded heartily. "Susanna and I are anxious indeed for any information and advice you can give us. We sense we have a most unusual situation here."

Calvin was shown to a chair. As soon as Susanna found something to amuse the children, she sat down near the man to learn what she could of the strange strain of humanity they had encountered at Epworth. And she was surprised at how fluent the unassuming Calvin could be when given a chance to talk.

"Why don't you go ahead and tell us what it is that's on your heart, Calvin," Samuel suggested. "We may break in with a question now and then."

"Well," the visitor began, "let me say first that Cora and I have lived here only two years. I'm working a piece of ground I inherited from my father's brother, although I don't remember ever having met him. As soon as I get it into better shape and we work out some problems with the authorities, we plan to sell it and move back to Glasgow."

"You may be sure we'll dislike losing you," said Samuel seriously, and Susanna nodded agreement. They could hardly have been more sincere.

"We are really on a big island here, you know, hemmed in by four rivers," Calvin continued. "Years ago it was a swamp, a haven for waterfowl, and the fishing was excellent. The natives had little connection with the outside world, and that was the way they wanted it. The swamp provided their living and the church took care of their social needs, so what else mattered?

Their island had had a long and bloody history of which they were only vaguely aware. What they did know was that they were at peace—no one was bothering them.

"Then the crown decided to have the area drained and made fit for agriculture. The idea was to help the people find a better life and be more productive."

Samuel held up a finger, signifying he wanted to break into the interesting narration.

"I think I know what's coming next," he said. "The people balked. They were not about to accept any kind of change."

"Exactly," Calvin agreed. "They were suspicious, and not entirely without cause. Anyway, they were not consulted when a Dutch engineer by the name of Vermuyden was contacted by the crown and authorized to drain the swamp. The only reason the people put up with the plan was they thought the engineer would be hiring a lot of help, and the men wanted to earn the extra money. The problem is that when Vermuyden began his operation, he imported all his helpers, and there were no jobs for the natives.

"At the same time, it was rumored that the territory was to be divided into three parts: one for the crown; one for Vermuyden, to compensate for his labors; the remainder for the people, who, theoretically, were to prosper by farming the rich, virgin soil."

"When was the thing finally settled?" Samuel asked.

"Ah, that's the stickler," Calvin answered. "It

has never been settled. The people refuse to give up possession of the ground being taken from them; and, while they are not equipped to rise up in arms, they do know how to get revenge. They pilfer and harass, showing their contempt in ways that are well nigh unbelievable among civilized people. Last summer they set fire to a field of flax that was ready to harvest. Their hatred is so intense, they have actually been known to cut the tendons in the legs of cattle that were brought here by Vermuyden's men—anything to let the innovators know they are not about to bow to their demands."

Susanna, whose sheltered life had not prepared her for what she was hearing, could hardly believe the shocking account that Calvin was giving.

"Surely," she observed soberly, "all these people are not like that."

"Oh, no," Calvin hastened to explain. "They all feel that they have been treated badly, but most of them are decent, God-fearing people who would live peaceful, productive lives if they were given the chance. You see, there is a rough element among them that is bent upon taking the law in its own hands. It is made up of a bunch of ignorant, brutish fellows; Cora calls them 'Latter Day Zealots.' Most of them have little understanding of what is right or wrong. They simply follow the leadership of their stronger, more militant peers, and do as they are told. I'm sure you saw a few of them come into church this morning."

"Go on," Susanna urged. "We may as well know the worst of what we face."

"Well," Calvin continued, "about all these troublesome fellows can do is make matters worse for everyone. It's too bad, but people on the outside tend to think that every native on the island is in harmony with, if not actually involved in, the vandalism."

"What is the answer?" she asked.

"I think," he responded slowly, "that some strong-willed person will have to assume leadership in educating the island people, and assist them in attaining their rights by lawful means. It may take years."

Calvin felt Susanna's clear blue eyes upon him, piercing the depths of his soul. He paused to let her speak.

"Perhaps God has sent my husband here to teach them the Commandments and show them how to keep them." She spoke with conviction.

"Ah, ha, you beat me to it, didn't you?" was Calvin's enthusiastic response. "That is exactly what Cora said today at dinner, except that she included you in the divine plan.

"Cora's smart," he added. "I know. I listen to her all the time."

Calvin grinned. Susanna neither smiled nor frowned, but there was something warm and sincere in her voice as she said, "Bring Cora with you next time. I want to know her better. Right now, I wish you would tell us more about yourselves."

"There isn't much to tell," he said. "Cora's

father was the Presbyterian pastor at the college church where I attended when I was in school. My foster parents were determined that I get an education. Cora and I both like the out-of-doors, so we became farmers, and we love it. We hope to make enough from the sale of our land here to stock our farm up north.

"By the way," he went on, "we have always favored merger between the Presbyterians and the established church. Do you folks think that will happen?"

Through most of this exchange, Samuel had been deeply involved in his thoughts. He had deep convictions, and he wanted to express them. Calvin's questions opened the way.

"We will have to wait and see," he answered simply. "The problem is bigger than the church, but it is not too big for God. It is bigger also than the trouble the people here are experiencing. The working classes all over Britain are involved, and education alone will never deliver them from their plight. For years the poor have been increasingly oppressed—objects of a growing exploitation—and one day their smoldering hatred will burst into flame."

Samuel was becoming both oratorical and evangelistic.

"Another revolution is on the way. In the midst of its bloody battles, orphaned babies, bloated with hunger, will be whimpering again by the roadsides, and the stench of rotting flesh will permeate the air from London to the farthest reaches of the land. It isn't necessary to paint pictures of the horrors; history has prepared us for them too many times already."

He paused for a breath.

"Then what is the answer?" Calvin asked.

"There must come a spiritual awakening," Samuel continued. "One that will sweep the empire, the continent, and cross the Atlantic; one that will leave neither death nor destruction in its wake, but life—an *inward witness of the Spirit* in the hearts of people everywhere, as they turn to God. It has happened before. It must happen again."

Samuel and Dr. Annesley had at one time discussed all this, and had been in full agreement. But Samuel was well aware that to many earnest, honest souls, including his own Susanna, it was just a dream. He was aware also that the Author of revival had in no wise endowed him with the spirit and talent necessary to set it in motion.

"I'm sorry," he said. "I didn't intend to preach a sermon. Revival will come. I may not live to see it, but I'm determined to do my best to help prepare the way, and I'll gladly stay right here to show these people that hatred and revenge will gain them nothing. I refuse to be intimidated!

"My interests, though, can never be confined to this small area," he added. "My parish is larger than this."

Calvin was a bit perplexed as he prepared to leave. Then Susanna helped relieve his mind with one brief statement:

"Samuel and I do not always agree on every point, but our goals are the same," she said. "You may be sure we are thankful for this better living the Lord has provided. We will do our best."

chapter 11

First Year at Epworth

Springtime is the year's most deceptive season. Ambitious people everywhere are prone to think of tilling the soil and caring for animals as merely pleasant diversions. Sammy's talents were of the head and heart, not of the hands, but before him lay the glebe. The thought of making it bud and bloom was delightfully daring. Other rectors had farmed it; he was certain that he could do it too.

Susanna was not so sure. "Where will we get the money?" she asked. "Farming the glebe will require the purchase of implements and livestock and seed. Don't forget that we need a riding horse in addition to our team, and we will have to go further into debt for that."

"But, Sukey," he argued, "not only will we raise all the cereals and vegetables we need for the table, and hay and grain for the animals, we will be able to pasture cows for milk and butter and raise pigs for meat. We can always market the excess. Of course, we will have to borrow money to do it, but we should have no trouble paying it back, since we will have no food to buy with our *living* and the income from my pen."

Susanna had to admit the plan had merit; so, reluctantly, she went along with her enthusiastic husband, and that day they extended their indebtedness to 200 pounds.

There was no time to waste, for planting time was upon them. So Samuel asked his new friend Calvin O'Conner, to help him purchase the equipment necessary to get started with the venture.

Calvin was more skeptical of the plan than Susanna had been, but he didn't feel free to say so. And later the neighbors laughed at Sammy's clumsy efforts with the plow.

Calvin and Cora were agreed that the new rector and his wife were fully capable of facing a stormy, uncertain future at Epworth, and equally incapable of compromising their principles. It was not easy to advise them, even though Samuel's apparent inability to successfully farm the glebe was distressing.

"We should have warned them," Cora spoke sharply as they considered the problem one evening. "It would have been ten times better if that city-bred Samuel had rented out the land. Then he could give full time to shepherding his flock and writing his poems.

"Let me read you something my father wrote

one time to the younger preachers of the presbytery," she said, as she reached for a book of notes she prized:

> Many country parsons learn too late that farmer folk are more than willing to keep the manse supplied with milk and honey, eggs and vegetables and meat, as long as they give themselves to the high calling of God. But once they divide their time and strength by producing these commodities for themselves, the gift horse turns its head.

"Yes, Cora," Calvin agreed, "your father was a brilliant man. You should have read that bit of advice to the rector. He probably wouldn't have listened, but we would feel better, wouldn't we?"

The second Sunday at church was not unlike the first. Samuel plainly positioned himself regarding the high moral standards God demands of his people. He condemned "adultery, fornication, uncleanness . . . hatred, variance, emulations, wrath, strife . . . envyings, murders, drunkenness, revelings, and such like. . . ." Each came up for denunciation in the uncompromising voice of the preacher. The reactions of the people were mixed; but the rector, who dared expound the Word of truth, was steadily becoming unpopular.

The consensus of the militant minority was that the only large thing about the rector was his mouth, and this assumption was strengthened by the fact that he was always congenial—even jovial—when he called upon the people. "Brave in the pulpit; scared of his shadow outside the church," the ruffians said. "Let him say the wrong thing on the street someday, and he'll wish he had never heard the name of Epworth."

But they misjudged him. They had heard his strong preaching but they hadn't considered his fighting-Irish blood. That is, until a day when he caught one of his farmer parishioners stealing corn from the tithe and appropriating it for himself. Suddenly the rector's congenial smile turned to rage and he accused the frightened fellow of robbing God.

"I'll put it back," the startled offender whimpered.

"Not here, you won't," cried Samuel, as he grabbed him by the wrist and marched him into town. There Samuel accused him publicly and left him at the mercy of the crowd. That day, rumors of the rector's cowardice were silenced forever, but his popularity was hardly enhanced by the incident.

A baby girl, christened Mehetabel—and called Hetty—came after only eight short weeks at Epworth. While Hetty was a happy, healthy child, Susanna, slow in regaining her strength, was confined to her room for several months. The time had come for Samuel to secure the assistance of servants, so two young women from town were formally interviewed. From her bed,

Susanna outlined their duties and structured stringent house rules with dignity and finesse— following, for the most part, patterns established by her mother years before. The maids, Dorcas and Hester, were instructed never to tolerate insolence or disobedience in the children, and to report all misdemeanors. Also they were to make themselves as inconspicuous as possible as they went about their duties, especially when guests were in the home. (This rule was necessary, no doubt, for hired servants constituted a luxury practically unknown in that area.)

The time had come also for Susanna to establish ordinances by which the children were to live. Samuel, Jr., at seven, was the proverbial good boy who never posed a problem. Emily, five, adored her brother and followed in his steps. Mother Susanna, depending on these excellent examples, determined early that no child of hers would be exempt from one jot or tittle of the code she was developing. She knew exactly how she wanted to rear her family, so every rule was put to the test with Sammy* and Emily, and they cooperated without a word.

Her basic philosophy of "training up a child in the way he should go . . ." was highly controversial. "Conquer the will," she said, "for self-will is the basis of sin. Since salvation is gained only through obedience to God, heaven and hell depending on this alone, a parent who indulges

*Her husband, thereafter, was called either Sam or Samuel, but never Sammy—since this was the name used for their son.

a child's self-will aids the devil. . . ."

In this, of course, Samuel did not concur. Susanna was aware of his opinion, and she recalled how she and her father had disagreed on this point also; but she was unbending.

It should be noted here that a redeeming factor in her legalistic fashion of rearing children was her own sweet, loving spirit. Unlike her husband, she never flew into a rage when a child was caught in an act of disobedience. Rather she calmly assessed the situation and firmly administered what she believed to be the proper punishment. Her children may have considered her to be overly strict, but they knew she was fair. And they loved her.

Included in her code were such interesting ordinances as follows:

> A child may cry, but softly. No loud crying will be tolerated, and no request will be granted one who cries to obtain it.

> The Ten Commandments shall be memorized by each child as early as possible and obeyed to the letter.

> There shall be no loud talking, noisy playing, or boisterous laughter. (Since Susanna never laughed, it was natural for her to curb it in others. In this, Samuel was not in agreement.)

> Bible reading and private prayer time shall be rigidly observed.

No child shall address another by the proper name without preceding it with *brother* or *sister*.

As soon as a child is old enough to sit at the table, he or she shall be restricted to three meals a day—no piecing between times.

At the table no child shall call out for anything, but whisper the request to the maid who will bring it to me.

No girl shall be taught to work until she has learned to read well. (While the emancipation of women was generally unheard of at that time, Samuel was in full agreement in this, as Susanna's father had been when she was a child.)

No child shall be punished or even chided twice for the same offense, and if and when a child confesses to a breach of discipline, no punishment shall be administered, thus removing the temptation to lie. (At this point Susanna was much more tolerant and expressed a greater degree of common sense than did her husband.)

There were many more rules, of course, all of which were carefully observed. Among them were those regarding the early elementary training of the children, beginning as soon as their little minds were capable of comprehending them. At this time, it was the intention of both

Susanna and Samuel to have the children tutored by professional teachers as early as was convenient. Then, in early adolescence, the boys were to be sent to boarding school, probably in London.

The months rolled by. At the approach of winter, troubles were piling high at the Epworth rectory. Samuel had learned that he was neither a tiller of the soil, nor a man of commerce. He hadn't known that farmers need reserves to carry them through the lean years and that the exorbitant interest rates of that era would make the luxury of borrowing money nearly prohibitive. The summer had been unusually dry; the glebe, considerably less productive than anticipated. A day of financial reckoning was fast approaching. Susanna was more aware and much more concerned about it than was her easygoing husband.

Adding to their difficulties, paradoxically, was a bit of good news. Some weeks earlier, Samuel had been highly honored with an invitation to preach at Gainsborough on the occasion of the bishop's visit to the area. He did well, which undoubtedly militated in his favor when a delegate was chosen to represent the diocese at Convocation in London.

Important matters relating particularly to the temporal economy and the spiritual welfare of the church at large were always under serious consideration at these high-level meetings. Samuel was anxious to see radical reforms in the latter area which, he believed, must precede and pave the way for a spiritual awakening. He could hardly have been more excited when this opportunity to voice his convictions and lend his influence in high places was extended to him.

Susanna was excited too, for she was always proud of her talented, impractical husband. While they differed in many matters, both theological and temporal, and the breach was widening every day, she never ceased to admire and love him.

The problem presented by Samuel's good fortune was centered in economics. The trip to London would cost 50 pounds per year. If he had been serving a city church where the honor and importance of his appointment were appreciated, this item of expense might be covered; but the Epworth people were reacting only with criticism of the extended periods he would be away.

It was a chilly day, and a relentless wind whistled at every corner of the house. Samuel was deeply absorbed in his writing, when he sensed that someone was standing in the doorway of his study. He turned to face Susanna. From the set of her jaw and the thin line of her lips, he knew he was in for a serious, unpleasant exchange, which he dreaded. She would be right, he would be wrong, and he'd have no good answers to the problem at hand. Of all this he was certain.

"Yes, dear," he said weakly.

"Samuel." He caught that inexplicable sting in her voice that he feared and detested. "What do you propose we do?" she asked. "It has taken every shilling we have received, from every source, to cover current expenses and pay the interest on our loans. The glebe has barely replaced the cost of the seed we purchased to plant it. Now you need expense money for Convocation, and our indebtedness still stands at 200 pounds."

"Shall I resign my appointment?" he asked meekly.

"No, you will not," she answered in the same steady voice, but the sting was still present. "That is an important part of your ministry, and the ministry is your calling.

"It will help if you can sell your poems, and we must cut back our expenses wherever we can. Both the house and barn are in need of repair, we are soon to have another child, and we're running low on fuel."

She paused, but since no word was forthcoming from her distraught husband, she continued: "We may have to dismiss one of the maids. . . ."

"Oh, no, we won't," he broke in firmly. "We may have to extend our indebtedness and hope for a better year ahead, but you must keep the girls. You cannot do their work."

Susanna started to answer, but she was cut short by a crashing, crushing, booming sound outside that resembled an explosion. Samuel bounced from his chair and ran to a window with Susanna at his side. They groaned. The rickety old barn had collapsed in the wind.

"We have no choice," Susanna whispered. "We must try to get another loan."

"When I get to London," Samuel answered, "I'm quite sure I can borrow 50 pounds."

The day for Samuel to pack his bags, mount the saddle horse he had purchased, and ride off to London for Convocation was drawing near. He and Susanna were together in his study again discussing the seriousness of their situation when the younger of the two hired maids appeared at the door.

"Come in, Dorcas," Susanna spoke kindly. "Is there a problem?"

"No, ma'am. Er, yes, ma'am, there will be," she stated nervously. "My mother is expecting a child later on, and she is going to need me. I'm telling you now, hoping you can get someone to replace me for awhile, if it doesn't inconvenience you too much. I'm awfully sorry."

"Of course, Dorcas," Susanna reassured her. "We will miss you, but we will make the necessary adjustment. You may tell your mother you will be with her."

With a word of thanks, the girl returned quietly to her duties.

"Well, Sam," Susanna was being matter-of-fact, "at least we will be spared the embarrassment of dismissing a maid if we have to do it."

Sam was sorry. "We'll find another girl," he said, "and we will manage to pay her."

Several days later, the post arrived with what seemed to be a temporary answer to their problem. The letter was from Samuel's brother, Matthew, who was in the throes of establishing his medical practice in London. It was brief and to the point, stating that their Aunt Aggie had passed away, and that Mother Westley, who was still quite strong and capable of caring for herself and more, would soon be forced to give up her house in London. Matthew suggested that one of the two brothers take her into his home, and the other provide ten pounds a year toward her support, the choice being left to Samuel. Matthew closed by saying he was glad to hear of the splendid living his brother had been awarded at Epworth.

"We will take her," Susanna said thoughtfully. "With Dorcas gone, she can look after the children and assist with lighter tasks around the house. Perhaps this is the Lord's way of helping us."

Samuel agreed, for he loved his mother, and the thought of having her in their home filled him with pleasant anticipation. He was not at all certain, though, that such an arrangement would remain satisfactory for any extended period. How his easygoing mother would get along with his exacting Susanna was yet to be seen.

There was another situation that worried him, too. Susanna, in all probability, would have her baby before his return from London.

"It's all right, Sam," she said. "I'm not without experience, for I've delivered eight already, you know. Cora O'Conner says there is a good midwife in town. I'll be all right."

Soon after Samuel's departure, the child was born prematurely and lived only an hour.

Susanna, slowly regaining her strength, was resting in her room. She missed Samuel, and while she probably wouldn't admit it even to herself, she enjoyed the peaceful days his absence provided. But she was not without her problems.

The youthful curate who was taking Samuel's place in the pulpit—an apprentice sent by the archbishop—was less than satisfactory in every way, and he had to be paid. The barn, which was badly needed, lay in a heap. And it would have to remain so, it seemed, until Samuel returned—for there was no money to hire men to rebuild it.

Dorcas reported that her mother was not well as she approached the days of her confinement, and she needed her daughter at once. Susanna allowed the girl to go, but her own condition was such that she was spending much of the time in bed. Hester was not complaining, but it was certain that the load placed upon the one loyal servant was more than she should bear.

Then, late one afternoon, when Susanna was assisting with the dinner, as was her practice, she heard the sound of wheels approaching the rectory. She went to the window, where, to her surprise and delight, she recognized Lacey and his wife assisting Samuel's mother from the rig. She went out to greet them. The back of the rig was stacked high with boxes.

As soon as the welcome visitors were unpacked and seated before the hearth with Susanna and her children, Lacey proceeded to answer many unspoken questions, while Hester added potatoes to the pot.

"Ya see, Sukey," he began, "your Samuel, bless his heart, honored us with a visit as soon as he arrived in London. We felt we owed him a big favor, we did.

"And we know too that we never could've repaid your father for his friendship through many hard years, even if he had lived to be a hundred. I guess you know his resources had pretty well dwindled before he died. What little he had, he properly left to your unmarried sisters and the two boys, but you may be sure he didn't forget his favorite daughter. He mentioned many times how you spent long hours in his study, poring over books that even he found tedious to read and hard to understand. Well, he wanted you to have his library, all of it, but he worried about getting it to you safely.

"Sure and you must have guessed already that the piles of boxes in the back of the rig contain those books, and they are yours, every one.

"When Samuel told us his mother would be going to Epworth, me lady and I decided to show a bit of our appreciation to both him and your late father by making the trip ourselves. We needed a holiday anyway, don't you know."

"Lacey takes it a little easy these days," his good wife added. "Now that our son has a team and rig of his own, he carries on the business, and he's doing well."

The old friends remained at Epworth for several weeks. Mrs. Lacey, large and strong, with a wholesome laugh and experienced hands, assisted Hester in putting the house into the best order. Samuel's mother was in a heaven of her own, caring for her obedient, beautiful grandchildren, leaving Susanna free to rest and regain her strength. Lacey, who never had difficulty making friends, induced Calvin O'Conner and a half dozen men from the church to rebuild the barn and pigsty, while he curried the horses, repaired the harnesses, fixed the fences, greased the wagons, and sharpened the plow. When the Laceys finally departed, the Epworth rectory, inside and out, was in excellent repair.

Susanna and her mother-in-law got along well on the surface—and actually liked each other—but they were miles apart on the matter of rearing children. Susanna demanded they keep the rules, while Grandma sneaked them bits of bread and butter. "Cry if you must, but softly," an unbending ordinance with Susanna, was a ridiculous breach of nature to the older woman. The opposing forces of mother and grandmother were both fun and frustrating to the children. It was good that Samuel returned when he did. Secretly, of course, he heard the complaints of both women, which made him an altogether unwilling, unhappy referee.

"Something ought to be done about this," his mother concluded softly.

"Something will have to be done about this!" demanded Susanna hotly.

"I'll take care of it, dear," he promised the latter, and he did exactly that.

Calling his mother into his study, he employed a bit of diplomacy clothed in Irish wit. "You certainly know how to bring up children," he said. "Just see what an excellent job you did with me."

She smiled her appreciation, then laughed at his audacity.

"But, Mother," he continued, "I have a problem that you never had to deal with. I'm married to Susanna."

She smiled again. "Yes, son," she said. "And I'm old enough to know better than to push into other people's business. I'm sorry. If Susanna will grant me a little time each day to tell the children stories, I promise to leave their discipline strictly to her. I wouldn't want to spoil them, would I now?"

So ended the Wesleys' first full year at Epworth.

chapter **12**
If Winter Comes . . .

It was early in the morning, January 1, 1700. A new day, a new year, a new century—all began with the same sunrise. Samuel Wesley was in his study while the family slept. He tried to write, but his thoughts disturbed him. *Why*, he wondered, *am I unable to sell my compositions?* All his life he had sold catchy, instructive, entertaining jingles; but at thirty-seven his pride prevented him from producing more such childish "literature." He failed to understand as others did that his serious "poetry" was only so-so, and pondered why hardly anyone would buy it. His prose productions were mostly well-researched articles, dealing with controversial issues that tended to get him into trouble. He really believed, though, that his *Dissertations on the Book of Job*, a work not yet begun—and one that would take years to complete—would finally bless the world and render him rich and famous. What it wouldn't do was pay those current bills that harassed him. Characteristically, he dismissed his depressing thoughts to dwell upon such riches as he could presently call his own. Therein lay the secret of his optimism. It never failed.

He considered first his wife of eleven perplexing years. While he and Susanna no longer tried to quit their quibbling, he loved her, and he never ceased to marvel at her ability to control her emotions and organize her forces. He could do neither.

Then there was Sammy, a handsome, serious-minded lad of excellent report who resembled his mother in every way. At ten, under her tutelage, he was academically far advanced for his years, and his father was teaching him Latin. Greek and Hebrew would follow shortly, for Sammy simply assumed he was called to the ministry and would be going on to Oxford.

Samuel smiled with pleasure as his thoughts turned to his oldest daughter, Emily, who had caused her parents not one moment of concern. She too was well along with her studies at a time when hardly another girl in all Lincolnshire could even write her name.

Next there was five-year-old Susanna, who enjoyed the advantage of having older siblings to give her an early start with her lessons. She adored her parents and especially her brother.

Mary, whose tiny deformed body often made her an object of ridicule by thoughtless children at the church, was a happy youngster nonetheless, and a favorite of her father's.

The youngest one, for the moment, was Hetty, a lively, pretty child of three, the delight of all the family.

After Hetty there had been two babies born and laid to rest, and now—as always, it seemed another child was on the way.

Where in all Britain, Samuel asked himself, *is there a man with a family equal to my own?* His musing turned to prayer. "Thank you, Lord," he prayed. "I am rich—extremely rich—but I need money to support my riches." Then in a spirit of intercession he prayed with fervor for those loved ones, until he heard Hester's call to breakfast. He had started the day well.

The past two years had wrought several changes in life at the rectory. Samuel's mother had returned to London; the O'Conners were back in Scotland; and Susanna had reorganized the household, assigning specific chores to each of the older children—retaining Hester as the only hired servant. A few of the people of the parish were becoming warm and friendly, but the "zealots" remained hostile, looking always for reasons to hound and harass the house of Wesley.

In January, the baby came, and Samuel's indebtedness had grown to 270 pounds, reaching the limit of his credit. He sat alone in his study, trying to concentrate. Only a dogged determination to meet his interest payments had saved him from serious trouble in the past; and the future was bleak—extremely bleak—for Susanna approached him just then about their situation.

"Whatever will we do?" she asked crisply. "We will be needing another thirty pounds within a month." She paused. "The archbishop helped us once. You must write him again."

"Please, not yet, Sukey," Samuel was hedging. "Calvin O'Conner once mentioned a farmer who used to attend the church, who loans money to his neighbors. He's something of a miser, I think, who lives off the exorbitant interest rates he charges. Perhaps I can borrow thirty pounds from him."

"But, Sam, how will we repay it?"

"Don't worry about that now, my dear," he answered, his optimism showing through. "We'll wade that river when we reach it."

The lender's name was Esau McTavish, a little man with a yellow beard that hid the hard, deep lines of his narrow, pinched countenance, accentuating a pair of cold blue eyes.

"Ye know now," he said, "these thirty pounds are due on demand the very minute ye're late with the interest."

Samuel mumbled his thanks as he took the money. He rode away quickly, for he was a good judge of character and he did not trust the mean, closed-fisted little fellow with whom he was forced to do business.

Several days later, Samuel was deeply absorbed in his study of Job, when his own patience as well as his ego received a crushing blow. Earlier that morning, Susanna and he had engaged in another of their little tiffs that were becoming much too common. They always tried to hide their troubles from the children, but Sammy and Emily were of such an age that nearly nothing escaped their notice. This time it was they who stood quietly in the doorway awaiting their father's attention.

"Welcome, children," he greeted them kindly. "Such somber faces tell me it's a most serious matter that brings you to my door this morning."

"Yes, Father," Sammy answered soberly. "Why don't you love Mother anymore?"

The startled man snapped to attention. "But, I do," he cried. "Your mother and I may disagree sometimes, but we love each other very much.

"You must have heard our petty quarrel this morning. Were you really so concerned?"

"We were scared," the boy responded. "We thought you were going to scream."

Poor Samuel! His little son had placed him soundly on the defensive, triggering instant anger. "I never argue with your mother when she starts throwing words at me quiet like," he said, fighting to control his feelings. "I'd rather she would scream at me; then I could scream back. Do you understand that?"

Emily answered, "Yes, Papa, but Mama's always right, isn't she?"

The man flushed red, which was warning enough for the children. They ran. Samuel's ire, as always, dissipated quickly, and he smiled to himself at Emily's audacity. But he was never to forget her simple rebuke.

He was reminded of it again one chilly, rainy morning in December when Susanna came once more to the door of his study. Her step was determined, her lips were drawn and firm, yet she spoke without undue emotion.

"Samuel," she said, "we have come to that river you said we would wade when we reached it."

The poor man dropped his gaze to avoid her piercing eyes. "Have we now?" he asked as casually as he could, for he detected that disturbing sting in her voice again.

"Yes," she answered. "There are exactly 4 shillings in our money drawer and we are still 300 pounds in debt. This may mean the debtor's prison for you, and something as bad or worse for the rest of us. And I hope you have not forgotten that another baby is due any day."

"I'm sorry, Sukey," he managed to say, "but what can I do?"

"I'll tell you what you can do," she answered in the same soft but spicy tone. "You can write the archbishop, as you should have done months ago, and explain our urgent need. Tell him that farming the glebe has been a failure and your writing brings almost no return. Remind him that I have borne eleven children—six of whom are still living—and that another one, in all probability, will arrive before he receives your message."

"Yes, dear, I'll write him today," came the plaintive promise.

"But that isn't all," she said. "Tell him that the repaying of old debts together with interest and taxes plus charities, including 10 pounds a year we send to your mother, which barely keeps bread on her table—all that, together with our household expenses, never fails to outweigh the modest stipend you receive."

"Do you really think I should write all that?" he asked.

"Of course you should." There was no hint of hesitation in her voice. "He will respond, for we have yet another reason for requesting assistance, and this one he cannot deny."

Samuel was having difficulty keeping up with her. "What are you referring to?" he asked.

"I'm referring to that new apprentice you've been saddled with," she answered simply.

"I'll write the bishop today, Sukey," he promised. "I'll tell him everything you say."

Tension in the rectory relaxed with the mailing of the missive, but the food supply was low. By careful rationing, however, Susanna was able to assure her loved ones that bread and broth would grace the family table for at least the better part of a fortnight. It was the lack of fuel in the dead of winter that posed a pressing problem.

"We have no choice," Samuel remarked with caution. "We must use the little money we have for coal."

"Four shillings will not buy much," Susanna answered, "but without it, the house will be cold by nightfall."

"Well," Sam admitted with a sheepish grin, "I do have ten pence tucked away for emergency. If we pool these meager resources, at least we will be warm for several days."

So it was that a blazing hearth added a touch of warmth in more ways than one to the home of the Wesleys that evening. And it was just in time, for late that afternoon, Susanna announced the beginning of labor pains, and the midwife who had assisted her before was alerted.

Samuel, as always on these occasions, took his place by his lady's side and tenderly held her hand. They were still in love, but it took sickness, accident, or childbirth to bring it to the surface. No word concerning their temporal plight was spoken as the hours crept by. Only the most pleasant of topics—their lovable children in particular—monopolized their conversation; and Samuel, nervous as expectant fathers always are, kept his fears under cover. But fears there were, for Susanna was suffering more than usual and the midwife stated frankly that there was "something different this time."

Finally a tiny baby arrived, but Susanna remained in deep distress. Samuel was nearly beside himself. "What can we do?" he cried.

"Nothing," the midwife answered calmly. "She's already doing it. There's another baby on the way."

It was nearly daybreak. The two tiny gifts from heaven and their mother were sleeping soundly, and Samuel, grateful for it all, sought a place of rest. He was awakened by the arrival of the post.

"Miracles!" he cried. "Miracles, I tell you—another gift from heaven!" A letter from the countess of Northhamton contained a generous gift of money. The bishop had shared the Wesleys' urgent appeal with her.

As soon as the ecstatic Samuel had shared the good news with Susanna, he went to his study and penned a note of appreciation to the archbishop. "My family is alive and well . . . ," he wrote. So was his extraordinary sense of humor, for he added, "Last night my wife brought me a few children, a boy and a girl, and I think they are all at present."

Even though the proverbial wolf had been driven back to the hinterlands for a season, there were many problems yet unsolved. Carrying the twins, along with her other burdens, had so weakened the overworked mother that she was forced to spend long weeks in bed. And the babies themselves were too weak to weather the earliest storms of life. First the boy then the girl slipped away, never to know the poverty and pain that haunted the rectory at Epworth.

Opposing political views never ceased to present a problem for the Wesleys. Samuel was a High Church Tory. He believed in the divine right of kings and was a loyal subject of William of Orange. Susanna, whose sympathies had always been with the Stuarts who were supplanted by William and his queen in 1688, was a confirmed Jacobite. To her, the Prince of Orange was a usurper of the crown. She was careful not to make an issue of it until one evening at family prayers when Samuel was petitioning the Throne of Grace in behalf of the king, she withheld her usual amen.

Later, in his study, Samuel reprimanded her severely, but she held her ground.

"If that be the case," he cried, "we must part. If we have two kings we must have two beds!"

Thereupon he saddled his horse and rode off in a huff, swearing never to return until she repented and asked his forgiveness.

Susanna remained firm. "Never," she said, "will I offend my conscience and my God by stooping to make an insincere confession."

Samuel, heavy of heart, hating himself for his impetuous ranting, was sorry he had denied the one he loved the right to think her own thoughts. But he was not sorry enough to turn his horse around and go back to her side and say so. (Samuel had business in London and his trip had already been planned.)

Of course I love Sukey and our children—I wouldn't leave them for the world, he mused as he jogged along in the saddle. *But I have to show them who is head of the house.* Then it was that he conceived an idea he believed would settle the matter quickly and in his favor. *I'll write to Susanna from Lon-*

don, threatening to apply for another chaplaincy and go back to the sea. He smiled at his craftiness. *I'll promise to support the family, but it shall be known that I refuse to live in a divided household.* Samuel had no difficulty convincing himself that he had stumbled onto a viable plan. *She'll be sorry.* He smiled again in happy anticipation. *She will beg me to come home.*

Back at the rectory, Susanna was reading Samuel's letter, and she longed to hear his voice. She cried when she read of his plan to return to the sea. She admitted to herself that she had been stubborn, and would gladly ask his forgiveness for that, if he would say he was sorry for his anger. She was prepared never to question his convictions again if, in return, she might be allowed to abide her honest opinions. Both Samuel and Susanna longed to settle their differences; but alas, they were miles apart in more ways than one.

Later, fire destroyed part of the rectory. Perhaps that helped to bring about their reconciliation.

In less than a year another boy was born; they named him John. Samuel and Susanna had hired a tutor for Sammy, but the fellow was given to excessive wine-bibbing, so they dismissed him, altering earlier plans for educating their boys. Another year rolled by and Sammy—quiet, brilliant, mature for his age—became proficient in languages due to his father's instruction. He excelled in other areas for having sat daily at the feet of the meticulous Susanna.

Now, at fourteen, he was leaving for London (Westminster) to pursue his studies. Tearfully he bade the family good-bye. While Susanna had wept with her loved ones at the graves of eight of her children, this separation came nearer than any to breaking her heart. However, it succeeded, fortunately, in strengthening family ties, for the future was fraught with trials and unspeakable misery.

Politics presented a problem for Samuel again. This time his trouble was with those militant members of his flock who despised his preaching. Violent threats became common, but Samuel brushed them aside as he pressed on "toward the mark for the prize of the high calling of God in Christ Jesus." He believed the ruffians would do him no actual harm.

In many ways, 1705 promised to be an excellent year. The glebe had never produced so well, the cows were giving more milk than the family needed, a magnificent field of flax was ripening beneath the summer sun, and Samuel had learned to wield a scythe. He planned to sell the grain to pay his interest and reduce his indebtedness. In the shade of the barn, he sat and sang as he sharpened the blade and repaired the cradle for a bountiful harvest. Then a friendly parishioner approached him with words of warning: "The opposition," he said, "is bent on driving you out of your church. You must be prepared to meet it."

Samuel kindly thanked the man for his concern, but, as always, he dismissed all thought of imminent danger. Yet real trouble lurked in the shadow this time, and that very night it came down full force upon him.

It was hard for Samuel to believe what Susanna was crying out to him as she shook him from his sleep. "Samuel, the glebe! It's all ablaze. Wake up! Everything will burn."

From the window, together they watched their field of flax burn as billowy waves of smoke rolled with the breeze. Neighbors were already on their way to fight the flames, lest their own fields be set afire by flying fagots.

Shortly after daybreak, the last smoldering vestiges of the destruction were being stamped out, but the crop was destroyed.

A sweating, soot-covered Samuel, having spent his energy fighting to keep the animals and the barn from yielding to the onslaught, was met at the door of the rectory by a sympathetic Susanna, who lovingly held him in her arms and wept.

"It's all right, Sukey," he said. "We must thank the Lord that only the crop was destroyed. We could be much poorer than we are, you know."

On Sunday morning the church was packed with people—most of them sympathetic, a few of them wearing devilish smirks, all of them awaiting Samuel's sermon—which they expected to be torrid, after the trauma the family had suffered.

Samuel surprised them. No preacher ever approached the altar with more grace, and never had Susanna been so proud as when he read the prayer and climbed the stair to the ancient pulpit. He took his text from the book of Job and developed his thesis with no particular display of emotion. Then, in the course of the message, he calmly discussed the problem which, he said, belonged not only to him and his precious family, but to the whole community.

"I am a man most blest this morning," he stated quietly, "for I have done no wrong for which my conscience might condemn me. The Lord is the only witness I call to my defense. Tragically, there are those less fortunate than myself, who will carry the scars of this black week to the end of life. Ironically, there are others who will wear their wounds through endless ages in fires—symbolic we presume—but no less devastating.

"What effect, you ask, has the incident had upon the rector of this historic shrine? Only this: I am determined to weather whatever storms may come, to face the winds of opposition with the fire of faith and the sword of truth, as long as strength and reason remain intact.

"I am aware that my words this morning will effect but little change in hearts and lives, and they shall soon be forgotten. It appears to be my lot to 'hold the fort' and 'bear the burden in the heat of the day.' Nothing less than another spiritual awakening—a visitation from heaven—will stir the nations and bring sinners to repentance.

" 'O Lord, revive thy work in the midst of the years,' " he cried.

"I have long contended that I may not live to see the great revival, but it will come."

Following the service, there were many who expressed real sympathy and swore allegiance to their pastor, but all were agreed that the evil ones had barely begun their mischief.

Esau McTavish, riding a bony, sway-backed horse, came into town demanding payment of the thirty pounds he had loaned the rector. The Wesleys had no money. The miserly McTavish was not a popular man in Epworth, and he found it awkward to present his claim. But a former friend of Samuel's, who opposed him politically, took advantage of the situation, and pressed the case against him. So, in full accordance with the law and the common practice of the day, Samuel was sentenced to an open-ended term in debtor's prison at Lincoln Castle. Susanna and the children wept as they clung to him and whispered their good-byes. Samuel wept too, for he was aware that the plight of his family was greater than his own.

That night the church was vandalized, and in the morning, when Hester went to milk the cows, she found them bawling with pain. The helpless, innocent beasts had been stabbed in such a manner that they could no longer give their milk.

Susanna went to her room alone to pray. She was faced with problems greater than she had ever known. Even so, her principal concern was for her husband. Since she had never seen a prison, she had no way of knowing what deprivation and suffering would be his to bear, and she realized again how much she loved him. Beneath his often stern exterior, he was a gentle, loving soul with a warmth of spirit that secretly, she had coveted all her life.

Susanna was utterly depressed. The only things of value in the household were several heirlooms and her jewelry. Never, even in the days of their severest poverty, had she or Samuel so much as mentioned these, for while their sentimental value could not be measured, their intrinsic worth was small enough. But this day she gathered them together and was preparing them for the post when Emily entered the room and saw what she was doing.

"Mother," the thirteen-year-old daughter cried. "Don't sell your jewels; you'll never get them back. We will get along—we always have, you know."

"I'm not doing it for us," Susanna whispered. "I'm sending them to your father."

In the prison, Samuel was busily cultivating the acquaintance of dejected men who shared his misfortune. His Irish humor made them laugh, and a tiny ray of sunshine began to glow amid the gloom. He invited them to join him in his prayers, and on Sunday morning he was allowed to conduct a service and preach a sermon. Some of the men, of course, refused to listen—until the day they saw Samuel weep and then return the jewels which might have bought his freedom. They *sensed* a sermon, a lesson in love that reached their hearts. From that moment Samuel was their chaplain.

The archbishop of York sat at his desk, burdened and perplexed. Before him lay two letters from Sam Wesley's political enemies, openly condemning him on several accounts. Neither of the self-appointed informers mentioned the harassment Samuel and his family had endured; but both letters ended rejoicing that the law had finally rescued "those precious people of Lincoln," from the "dishonorable despot" who had posed as their pastor and friend.

Another letter, this one from the rector himself, lay unopened. The archbishop had known the Wesleys in earlier years, and he liked them. In recent months he had received urgent financial appeals from Samuel, to which he had responded without investigation.

Perhaps I was wrong, he mused as he proceeded to open that third letter, expecting to find a fiery defense of the rector's position, a condemnation of the people of his parish, as well as another request for money and for an appointment to a stronger church of enlightened people who would appreciate his scholarship.

Samuel's letter, however was delightfully different from that which the bishop expected.

My Lord,
Now I am at rest, for I have come to the haven where I've long expected to be. . . . I was arrested in my churchyard. . . . The sum was not thirty pounds but it was as good as five hundred. Now they knew the burning of my flax, my London journey, and their throwing me out of the Regiment had sunk my credit and exhausted my money. . . . One of my biggest concerns was my being forced to leave my poor lambs in the midst of so many wolves. . . . My wife bears it with that courage which becomes her, and which I expected from her.

I don't despair of doing some good here [in prison] . . . for I have leave to read prayers every morning and afternoon and to preach once on Sunday. . . . And I am getting acquainted with my fellow jailbirds as I can; and shall write to London next post, to the *Society Propagating Christian Knowledge*, who, I hope will send me some books to distribute among them. I should not write these things from a jail if I thought your grace would believe me ever the less for my being here; where if I should lay my bones, I'd bless God and pray for your grace.

> Your most humble servant
> S. Wesley

The archbishop was deeply moved by Samuel's characteristic optimism and genuine Christian spirit. He could hardly have been more sympathetic as he proceeded to carry on a friendly correspondence with his "pastor in prison," through which he learned all the gruesome details of the trouble. He even made a trip all the way to Epworth to visit Susanna and her children, leaving them a generous gift of money.

Then when the truth of the matter was spread abroad, friends rich and poor, many of whom remained incognito, came to the aid of the family. More than half of the longstanding indebtedness was graciously covered by gifts, and a satisfactory arrangement for liquidating the remainder was established.

Samuel, released from debtor's prison, returned to Epworth. He was met at the door by Susanna, whose joy was overflowing.

"I love you, my husband," she said. "I hardly know what to say or do."

Samuel smiled, recalling her words on the occasion of their betrothal.

"I think," he said, quoting her exactly, "it would be perfectly proper for you to take me in your arms and kiss me."

In the days that followed, Samuel and Susanna resumed their heavy schedules, but Saturdays were set aside for rest and relaxation as in their early days at Holburn. They took long walks down country lanes together and peace—precious, priceless peace—prevailed.

chapter **13**
The Red Brick Rectory

One chilly night in February 1709, the Epworth
rectory burned to the ground. Twelve-year-old
Hetty, asleep in a tiny attic bedroom, was awakened when a brand of burning thatch fell upon
her bed. The terrified lass ran to the window and
shouted, "Fire!" to the blackness without, where
fortunately some errant townsman, staggering
home from the local pub, heard her cry and
spread the alarm. Hetty awakened her father
and mother. Susanna, eight months pregnant
with her nineteenth child, lifted baby Charles
from the cradle and began mumbling something
about the money box in which their entire fortune of twenty pounds was hidden.

"Forget it," Samuel cried as he pushed her to
the top of the staircase that was already beginning to burn. "Save yourself and Charlie. I'll

help rescue the other children, and the money too, if I can."

Hetty had roused Emily and the servants, who were carrying the tiny ones and leading the other children toward the stairs. Samuel heard Hester calling, "Follow close behind me. I'll not let you get hurt," and he began whipping back the flames that were swiftly closing off the only avenue of escape. The front entrance through which Susanna had pushed her way, sustaining burns on her arms and legs, was all ablaze; so Samuel directed the others to turn sharply at the foot of the stairs and run toward the back of the house. Moments later they were seen tumbling out through windows and the side door to the garden. Neighbors were already arriving, and women were caring for baby Charles and Susanna, who had collapsed on the ground.

Samuel gathered his shivering family together to be sure all were accounted for, but alas! *John was missing*. Without a word he reentered the house to face the fiery blast. The staircase, by then a roaring furnace fed by the draft from the gaping entrance, was a solid mass of flames. Samuel's hopes were shattered. Back in the garden he fell to his knees commending the soul of his son to God, unaware of a near-miraculous drama unfolding around him.

John Wesley was a wiry five-year-old boy who did everything: work, play, study, even sleep, as though his last opportunity had arrived—which, this time, was truly the case. Hester's screams had failed to rouse him, but the hot smoke burning his nostrils finally brought him to his senses. The startled lad poked his tiny head out from behind a curtain to see flaming fingers of fire crawling up the walls and across the ceiling. He ran to the top of the blazing stairs and back into the room again. Beneath a window stood a large chest upon which he had often sat to watch the rain and the snow, and he quickly climbed upon it. He gazed out upon the confusion in the garden. In the eerie light cast by the fire he saw his father on his knees in prayer, and his mother lying on the ground as still as death. Great tears blurred his eyes as a sense of loneliness bordering on desolation and an awful fear of fire possessed him.

That's how he was when Hester, who loved him more than all the others, caught a glimpse of his face at the window.

Near her stood a group of men wanting to help, but helpless. She recognized one large fellow called Franklin, a friend of Samuel's. She grabbed his arm and began, hysterically, to beat her fits against his breast, shouting incoherently.

"What do you want?" he cried, as he laid his big hands on her shoulders and held her struggling at arm's length.

"He's alive!" she wailed. "I saw him at that window! Get a ladder. . . ." The poor girl fainted, falling into the arms of Franklin's wife.

"It's too late to find a ladder," the tall man shouted. "I'll lean against the wall and you men help someone up onto my shoulders. Maybe we can reach him."

After one unsuccessful attempt, they did indeed boost a smaller fellow upward into place, and he grasped the window sill. A moment later, little John was in his arms; but the man was helpless, standing unsteadily on Franklin's giant frame.

"Drop to your knees, Franklin, steady now, so they won't fall," one of the men instructed. "Then he can drop the boy into our arms."

Just as the maneuver was accomplished, the roof fell in, and a billion blazing bits of tinder, like a galaxy of stars, burst forth against the wintry sky.

Susanna had regained consciousness, and Samuel, nearly beside himself with joy, hurried to her side.

"Family, friends," he cried. "Let the house go. I am rich enough! Let us kneel together and give thanks to God."

The church then decided to build a substantial rectory of red brick, large enough to properly house a large family, and one which wind or fire would not be likely to destroy. Such a project was to require at least a year to complete, and this posed an immediate housing problem for the Wesleys. There was no place where the family could all live together.

Samuel and Susanna with baby Charles were provided comfortable lodging in the town. Emily, who was seventeen, stayed with them to care for her mother, who, in less than a month, gave birth to another girl. They named her Kezziah and called her Kezzie.

Of the nineteen children she had borne in twenty years (including the two sets of twins), nine had been laid to rest. Now most of the survivors were to be temporarily scattered near and far. The servants were necessarily dismissed, but the faithful Hester quietly arranged for the younger children—except little John—to be given homes by friendly parishioners. She wanted to keep John herself, but having no way to do it, she prevailed upon a pastor of her acquaintance in another village to take him.

"He's special," she told the parsonage lady as she brought the sparkling five-year-old to the door. "It's important that he doesn't pick up the coarse manners of the people around Epworth. I'm so glad you folks are willing to make this sacrifice."

"Willing? Sacrifice?" the woman responded as she stooped down to hug the lad. "I wish we could keep him forever. God has not blessed my husband and me with a family, you know."

There were two substantial homes in London that played important roles in the lives of the Wesley girls.

One was that of Matthew Westley, who by then had become a successful man of medicine. He was unaware of his brother's financial difficulties, although his mother, upon her return to London, had tried to enlighten him. He, too, understood the problems caused by the fire and offered to shelter Hetty, who was twelve. Hetty, the most vivacious of the Wesley girls, had inherited characteristics of both her parents. Like her mother, she was beautiful and brilliant, but the resemblance ended there. Her winsome wit and lilting laughter, her love for people, and a flair for verse—which, in her case, ripened into poetry of genuine merit—had their roots in her father, Samuel.

The second refuge was the home of Samuel Annesley, Susanna's brother, a successful man of business. He recalled the pleasant times he and his brother, with their sisters and friends, had enjoyed in the old days at Spital Yard. He had loved and admired Susanna, and he had never forgotten the knowledgeable, congenial Sam Westley who had paid weekly visits to their home and later married his favorite sister.

He had met Sam again when Convocation brought him to London; and needing an honest man to handle some investments, he gave Sam the job. Samuel did his best, but not being a man of business, he invested poorly, sustaining losses for his brother-in-law which brought about a breach in what had been a good relationship. However, when Annesley heard about the fire, he offered to take one of the girls until a new house was built; and the young Susanna, who had just turned fourteen, was sent to him. Before the year ended, however, he went to India where he amassed a fortune. The girl was sent to stay with Hetty.

Back at Epworth, the beautiful new rectory was under construction. So, thirteen months after the fire had destroyed everything—furniture, clothing, books, papers, accounts, even many important church records—Samuel and Susanna, empty-handed, were ready to move into their new home. They had no choice but to go into debt again for bare necessities, but they had learned their lessons well.

It was agreed that Susanna would keep the accounts and purchase clothing and furniture as funds became available. At least Susanna had a house, second to none in the parish, in which to rear her family. The first floor had a large kitchen and dining room, a spacious parlor and a study. The second story was divided into bedrooms, and a mammoth finished attic completed the new abode.

Like most of their neighbors, the Wesleys were still forced to live at the poverty level, even though Samuel's writings were beginning to sell. Soon the servants returned to their duties, however, making it possible for Susanna to reorganize her family and set up her school.

Poor meticulous Susanna! She was shocked at the sloppy habits and uncouth language her young ones had acquired during their year away from home. She was fully capable of correcting these infractions of her rules, but she couldn't cope with changing attitudes in Hetty and young Susanna. Their stay in London had opened a whole new world to them. They came home asking for expensive coats and shoes and dresses, and exhibiting a radically relaxed life-style—all of which had been theirs to enjoy in the homes of their doting uncles.

"But we have no money for luxuries," Susanna tried to explain, "and anyway, such things are not important."

It was hard for her to be convincing, for she had not been plagued with poverty in her own childhood. She had no qualms, however, in re-establishing the exacting rules of conduct she had imposed earlier upon her family. Actually, Samuel was the more lenient parent at this point; but the girls blamed him—not their mother—for their woes, and they were not entirely wrong.

Life in the new rectory was much better than it had been in the old one. Susanna's extended illnesses were past, and her childbearing days were over. She and Samuel continued to disagree on many issues, but they learned to live and love in spite of it.

The classes Susanna conducted in the rectory were in session six hours a day, incorporating all the rules and regulations so sternly observed in private schools of early eighteenth-century England. Susanna, however, was able to maintain nearly perfect discipline without the inhumane floggings to which frustrated schoolmasters were known to resort. In addition to observing the regular classroom activities, she set aside one hour a week for private consultation with each child, dealing particularly with their individual problems, as seen in the light of exemplary

Christian living. It was in these sessions that she impressed upon their receptive minds her firm conviction that "Salvation is gained only through obedience to God; heaven and hell depending upon this alone. . . ."

The children were at least vaguely aware that she and their father were not in agreement on this point; but their confidence was in their mother, who never failed to "practice what she preached," and whom they admired and loved supremely.

Education in the home did not end with Susanna's instruction, however. Samuel was a classical scholar of distinction, and he happily made himself available to any of the children who wished to pursue Latin, Greek, and Hebrew. Most of the girls, as well as John and Charles. wanted to extend their education as far as possible, probably because of Susanna's ability to make learning an enjoyable experience.

It is not to be assumed that life in the rectory was all work and no play. Susanna remembered well the good times her brothers and sisters and friends had had around the big table at their games in their father's house. So she arranged for her children to have their hours of fun; and, strangely enough, she became more involved in their games than she had been in those at Spital Yard when she was a child.

By 1712 the younger children were reaching their formative years. It was her daughters for whom Susanna was most deeply burdened. The two older ones had reached the marrying age at a time when "a good match" was about the only means of security and hope of happiness available to young women. The Wesley women had the beauty, charm, and graces (if not the clothes) necessary to attract men of most excellent report. But where, in the fenlands around them, were such eligible males to be found? Young farmers who could barely read and write could hardly expect to be paired with young girls studying Greek and Latin who had no knowledge of the hardship that rural married life might impose upon them.

Susanna saw clearly that her daughters were headed for dreary days of disappointment, while the boys faced futures beautiful and bright. Such was the culture, the situation in which they lived—and the stern Victorian age still lay ahead.

John was nine, a methodical lad who, hour by hour, reasoned his way through every crisis great and small. His father said in effect that he believed their Jackie would not so much as respond to the call of hunger or thirst without first having found sufficient reason for doing so. However, John was a lively lad and always a star student in his mother's incomparable academe, as Samuel called her school. His personality resemblance to his mother was almost uncanny. An outstanding ability to organize himself and others, a natural talent for leadership, and a carefully disciplined personal life made him almost a copy of her as a child.

Charles Wesley was five, and owing to an agile

mind and unusual opportunities to learn, he was already reading and writing, adding and subtracting, and forever raising his hand to answer questions that Susanna was directing to the older children. He was short and stocky, quick-tempered, witty, and extremely personable, resembling his father in every way. He and John were as different in temperament as were their parents, but the two boys could hardly have been better friends. So the one great disappointment of Charles' childhood came when John, at the tender age of eleven, was sent to Charterhouse, a famous preparatory school in London, with Oxford as his goal.

At a farewell party given by Susanna in John's honor, Hetty, whose favorite sibling was little Charles, saw him sneak away alone to their father's study. A few minutes later, when he didn't return, she went in and found him crying.

"Why, Charles," she said, "you should be happy for your brother. Don't you see what a good time the rest of us are having?"

He dried his eyes.

"I know you can't help feeling the way you do," she continued, "but can't you pretend you are glad for John and his wonderful opportunity to study?"

"I guess so," the boy answered, and together he and his sister returned to the party. Charles didn't know it, but Hetty was covering her real feelings too as she laughed and sang, fulfilling her role as "the life of the party."

At sixteen she was the most beautiful of the

Wesley girls: personable, brilliant, talented—and unhappy. Beneath her ready smile lurked a deep resentment approaching rancor, hurts that knew no healing, hidden hostility that bordered on hatred. She wasn't jealous of John that evening—only envious of those opportunities that the accident of birth was laying at his feet. Since a subordinate role with no possible avenue of escape was being imposed upon her by gender alone, her anger was directed toward her father, whom she resembled and secretly admired. When he bragged about his boys and discussed their brilliant futures, she cringed with jealousy. Hers was never an outward hostility; she left the luxury of that to Emily, who was vocal in her criticism of her father. Since both girls loved and sympathized with the calm, long-suffering Susanna, they felt justified in planning a subtle revenge on the quick-tempered Samuel. Theirs was a long-range plan.

The girls were unable to understand why their parents would permit, if not actually arrange for, a child to leave the loving care of family and friends at the early age of eleven. So, just three years later, when Samuel insisted upon sending eight-year-old Charles to Westminster to live with Sammy, Jr., and attend school there, they felt the time had come to carry out their well-laid plans.

So it happened that one December morning in 1716, while the family was still trying to get accustomed to life without good-natured Charlie around, Hetty and Emily came screaming down the stair, crying, "Ghost! There's a ghost in the house!"

"All right, all right," Samuel tried to calm the girls. "There are rats in the attic, I know."

"This wasn't a rat." Hetty stated boldly. "He rapped on the head of our bed until we were both awake. Then every time we moved, he rapped again. He was determined that we would know he was in our room."

Little Kezzie was so frightened she could barely keep her teeth from chattering long enough to ask, "How do you know it was a he?"

"Oh," Emily answered quickly." You could tell by the heavy rap. Just for fun I called him Jeffrey and he rapped louder than ever."

There was indeed a great mystery surrounding the "appearance" from time to time of "Old Jeffrey" at the rectory. Details involved in the account naturally became exaggerated until no one knew for sure which reports were mere figments of the imagination. Belief in the existence of ghosts was common at the time, which may explain Susanna's acceptance of the mystery of the poltergeist.

The theory that Hetty masterminded a hoax, while Emily, and others perhaps, assisted her in carrying out the eerie details, is not unlikely—for the "ghost" reflected the strong prejudices of the girls. It was kind to Susanna, honoring her request not to be disturbed during the hour of her private devotions. Politically, it was diametrically opposed to Samuel's dogmatic positions, rudely interrupting his prayers for the king. Old Jeffrey was purported to possess an element of gallantry, lifting latches and opening doors, but only at the approach of the girls. Even though Hetty and Emily maintained the apparition was a male, they expressed no fear, and apparently experienced no embarrassment over his nocturnal visits to their bedroom. Lastly, Samuel, who never gave more than partial credence to the supernatural element in the goings-on, thought it barely possible that Sammy, Jr., had died and was trying to gain the attention of the family. When he demanded to know if this were true, the noises ceased and soon the ghost was heard from no more.

Why the girls, if they were indeed perpetrators of a hoax, never confessed it, is an unanswered question. It has been suggested, however, that the "little game" got so completely out of hand that they agreed never to disclose the truth; hence it lies with them forever in their graves.

Now that the family was reduced in size and there were grown girls to lighten Susanna's load, she and Samuel got back on the old schedules they had developed in Holburn. Each one carried on private correspondence with their sons. Samuel spent three hours on Monday and Tuesday mornings assembling his notes on the book of Job and began the long, tedious work of writing (in Latin) what he believed would be the crowning achievement of his life.

And poverty continued to prevail in the beautiful red brick rectory at Epworth.

chapter **14**
Opportunities and Setbacks

Except for the specter of insufficient finances (an omnipresent ghost that was altogether too authentic), life at the rectory was running smoothly. Samuel had never enjoyed such excellent rapport with the people of the church, and he was fully aware that he owed the "swing to the better" to Susanna. During Samuel's last trip to Convocation, the curate whom he had hired to take charge of the services had begun to lose his audiences. The people didn't like him, and he was not a good preacher. At the same time, since there was no Sunday evening worship, Susanna held services in the rectory kitchen for the benefit of her children. Soon they were inviting their friends, who in turn brought their parents, and the assembly began to mushroom. Where she seated, or otherwise stationed, her congregations is something of a mystery—for according to her own account, attendance soon approached the two hundred mark.

The curate became irate. He was preaching to less than fifty people on Sunday mornings in the church; so he wrote a scathing letter of complaint to Samuel in London. Sam was sympathetic with his man. After all, he was a strict conformist, and the idea of a woman performing priestly functions was unthinkable. So he wrote to Susanna relating what he had been told. He asked her kindly to discontinue her ministrations, if indeed the report were true. The next day, he followed with a stronger note of disapproval.

Her answers were masterpieces of expediency. Excerpts from her letters read as follows:

> As I am a woman, so I am also mistress of a large family. And though the superior charge of the souls contained in it lies upon you as the head of the family and as their minister, yet in your absence, I cannot but look upon every soul you leave under my care as a talent committed to me.

> As for your proposal of letting some other person read ... I do not think one man among them could read a sermon without spelling a good part of it, and how would that edify the rest?

> Our meeting has wonderfully conciliated the minds of this people toward us. ... If you do after all think fit to dissolve this assembly, do not tell me you desire me to

do it, for that will not satisfy my conscience, but send me your positive command in such full and express terms as may absolve me from all guilt and punishment for neglecting this opportunity of doing good when you and I shall appear before the great and awful tribunal of our Lord Jesus Christ.

That did it. The meetings continued, and later, Sunday evening worship services were installed in the church to replace them.

Time was slipping by, and one by one the girls were leaving home. Anne, of whom little is known, was the first one to marry, and it was said that she and her husband lived happily together. Later, daughter Susanna went to London to visit her Uncle Matthew, where she met and married a man of wealth without consulting her father and mother. This turned out to be a tragic marriage in every sense, which added to her parents' concern for the rest of the girls. Emily found employment at a boarding school in Lincoln and soon was given full supervision of the children. This left only four girls at home, of whom Hetty was the oldest. Martha, eighteen, was a pleasant, unsmiling, affectionate, dependable girl, who, like her brother John, was the image of her mother. Then there was lovely, pretty Mary who, with the others, had endured every problem that poverty and privation had pressed upon the parsonage, plus a physical deformity that often made her an object of ridicule. She was the one who might have been bitter, but no word of complaint ever escaped her. Kezzie, the youngest, was never strong. She decided early to remain single, stay at home, and care for her parents in their declining years.

Samuel was sitting in his study; his weighty notes on the book of Job lay in neatly arranged piles before him. For months, Hetty had been serving as his secretary and everything was in perfect order. During this period, a congenial father/daughter relationship developed. The two were intellectually compatible, and never had they enjoyed so many things in common. But that morning, during a frank discussion, feelings were hurt and the daughter left her father's study in a huff.

Hetty had been offered a position as governess by a wealthy family in Kelstein, where she would be surrounded with luxury, could earn her own living, buy nice clothes, and be free from the parental authority she had always detested. Both Samuel and Susanna had agreed that she should go, but her father had mixed emotions regarding the move. His unmarried daughters would always remain in "early adolescence" in his thinking, and Hetty had just turned twenty-five. However, his parental authority had not been exercised without a measure of reason. For years, Samuel and Susanna had been concerned with Hetty's apparent weakness for men, manifested in a coquettishness that may have seemed harmless to many of her friends. But coupled with her flirty ways was a dangerous naivete—she was easily swayed by pretty words of praise.

Samuel, especially, was aware of the danger, as he had a keen understanding of men. Seldom was he mistaken in his appraisal of a stranger. Only recently, Hetty had become enamored of a man who had been assisting him at the church. Samuel had dismissed the fellow, for he sensed his insincerity and had reason to believe his intentions regarding Hetty were trifling at best. Hetty had reacted angrily, but she soon realized that her father's judgment was valid, for her "friend" turned his attention to another and thereby proved himself dishonorable.

Samuel was meditating upon all this as he sat alone, and a feeling of sadness enveloped him. He loved his daughters no less than he did his sons; but the only way he could express that love was to assist Susanna with their education while attempting to protect them from evil-minded males and seeking to insure that they married well. Unfortunately, the need and sensibilities of women were beyond his grasp. He was utterly devoid of diplomacy in dealing with his daughters. His girls loved and admired him, but they had never been able to cope with his quick temper and harsh manners. Their calm, clear-thinking, pleasant, unsmiling mother was much easier to live with. It had always been so.

Now that Hetty was preparing to leave home, Samuel was sorry they had argued. He was glad, though, that he had expressed his concern and talked plainly of the weaknesses he saw in her. That, of course, had made her cringe; but her father felt sure she would remember his counsel, and never could she say she had not been warned.

Samuel was roused from his contemplation, sensing that he was not alone. He turned to face Susanna, who was standing in the doorway, but this time there was no sting in her voice as she addressed him. Through all the hard years she hadn't lost her beauty, and he, looking lovingly into her clear blue eyes, told her so. She placed a soft hand on his shoulder and bent down to kiss him.

"Perhaps we should discuss our future, Samuel. It's waiting out there, you know, and we will have to face it."

"There's no way I can argue that, Sukey. Tell me, what brought this to your mind so suddenly?"

"Maybe you haven't noticed," she reminded him, "but we are beginning to grow old."

"Yes, we are. Lately I have become aware of that. In a few days I'll be sixty, but what can we do about it?"

"Well, dear, Martha will soon be leaving home, no doubt, and there will be only four of us left in this big house. You have been rector here for twenty-five years. Why don't you ask for an easier field where you can complete your ministry?"

"I've thought about that, Sukey, but I can't induce myself to do it. Our years here have not been easy ones, but we have witnessed miracles of grace. The ruffians who harassed us in the early days are gone, and the people here are our friends. Much of the credit for that belongs to you, I know.

"I have always felt that a great awakening lies in store, and the conviction is stronger now than ever."

"I know, dear," she answered. "You have told me that many times. And you will be pleased to know that I settled something very important a long time ago."

"What was that?" he asked.

With love, she recited: " 'Whither thou goest, I will go, and where thou lodgest, I will lodge; thy people shall be my people and thy God, my God. Where thou diest, I will die and there will I be buried. The Lord do so to me and more also, if ought but death part you and me.' "

Susanna failed to share her husband's hope for a sweeping revival, but she wisely kept her own counsel. She tended to favor the philosophy of certain theologians who believed the world was getting better—slowly, to be sure, but improving, nonetheless. They believed that someday "Peace on earth, good will towards men," as an accomplished task, would usher in a reign of "Righteousness, peace, and joy in the Holy Ghost." At least there was an element of logic in that view to support her contention that one can only be saved by universal obedience, by keeping all the laws of God, heaven and hell depending upon this alone. Thus she had taught her children, and up to this time, her success had been phenomenal. Likewise, the moral tone of the Epworth population was clearly on the rise.

The next two years passed quickly. Martha had found employment away from home; Hetty was doing well with her work as governess; and the big house seemed terribly empty. Hester too had surprised the family with an announcement of her engagement to a highly respected farmer—a member of the church—who had lost his wife the winter before. But, as always, a growing indebtedness plagued the Wesleys.

Samuel and Susanna were assessing the situation as they had done at least a hundred times during their twenty-seven years at Epworth. It was one of those torrid, sultry days in July when even the luxury of a little breeze was being denied them.

"Whatever will we do?" Susanna asked, wiping away great beads of perspiration.

Samuel was pleased to note the lack of sting in her pathetic voice, and his indigenous optimism was not about to fail him.

"Now, now, Sukey; something good will happen. It always does, you know."

In that moment, as though his words were pure prophetic utterance, the post arrived with a letter from the archbishop. Samuel tore open the seal and read the missive. It said simply that, for some time, a better living in a more affluent area had been under consideration for Samuel;

but since the rector now had the full confidence of his people and the church was doing well, it appeared to be the better part of wisdom for him to remain in charge of the work at Epworth. It went on to say, however, that the church at Wroot, less than five miles across the swampland, would soon be without a pastor, so this second living was being offered to him.

"Does this mean we shall move to Wroot?" Susanna asked.

"Of course we will, Sukey. The rectory there is small, but it will do nicely for our dwindling family, and that additional salary will supply our needs and more. We will rent out this big house, and that will pay for a curate to assist with the services. Finally, we will be able to free ourselves of debt and save some money."

Susanna wondered, but she was glad for the opportunity.

The people at Wroot welcomed the Wesleys with open arms. They had never had a pastor with equal grace and talent, nor a parsonage lady as personable, knowledgeable, and kind. Samuel had learned his lesson—he didn't so much as plant a row of radishes to hinder him in his duties as their spiritual leader. And the people never failed to keep the larder at the rectory stocked with food. Samuel and Susanna could hardly have gotten off to a better start. And the end, so it seemed, was not yet.

Susanna had been corresponding with her

brother, Samuel Annesley, in India, who, in response to her appeal for help, wrote that one day soon he would return to England. Then, he intimated, he would see that her every need was bountifully supplied. She was led to believe that he planned to give her a thousand pounds.

Hardly had the furniture been arranged in the rectory at Wroot, when a notice appeared in a newspaper stating that Mr. Samuel Annesley was expected in London on or about a given date, on one of his company's vessels. Dear Susanna was so elated that, for once, she could hardly contain her feelings. For the first time in her married life, she expressed a hope of having her evening years blessed with prosperity and peace.

She made arrangements to go to London to meet her brother at the dock. It would be her first trip back to the city in thirty-five years.

Disappointment and sorrow had been a way of life for Susanna and, sadly, this was not about to change. First, upon her arrival in the great metropolis, she learned that her friends, the Laceys, had grown old and died. Their son, however, welcomed her to town and made his rig available to her at any time. She was anxious to see her sons, Sammy and Charles, who lived in Westminster, and John planned to come from Oxford to meet them there. But since her brother's ship was already docking, young Lacey took her immediately to the pier.

Alas! There had been foul play and her brother was not aboard, nor was he ever heard from again. His fortune, too, had been confiscated.

Young Lacey, sensing Susanna's sorrow, did his best to add a bit of pleasure to her journey.

"Before I take you to your sons," he said, "I think it will be well to show you some of the old landmarks you remember."

Susanna was grateful for his concern and asked to see her old home at Spital Yard. She wept as they stood by her parents' graves, and later marveled at the grandeur of the new St. Paul's Cathedral. Among many points of interest, they visited the Church in Holburn where Samuel had served as curate; even the little apartment into which she and Sam had moved the day of their wedding. Lacey took her into the country to beautiful Bunnhill Fields, the burial place of many eminent Puritans, including John Bunyan, whose *Pilgrim's Progress* was already becoming a popular work.

Not far away stood an old deserted building. Lacey called her attention to a pile of broken rocks and mortar on the ground beside it.

"That debris," he said, "is what remains of the old St. Paul's Cathedral. Mr. Wren, the architect, arranged to have it carried away and dumped there, where it is slowly sinking out of sight in the spongy swamp. I helped haul tons of it, myself, when I was a young man. That old building beside it was a foundry where cannon barrels were cast, until an explosion partly destroyed it."

"All a part of God's plan," observed Susanna. "One day, those cannons will be beaten into plowshares."

Susanna was much too strong to allow one more disappointment to spoil her happy reunion with Sammy and Charles, even though John, unfortunately, was unable to meet with them. Sammy was the heard usher (teacher) at Westminster School, a position he had held from the time he graduated from the university. He had been almost a second father to John, and especially to Charles.

Sammy, always a favorite of his mother's, took whole days off from his heavy responsibilities to be with her.

"Tell me the truth about John and Charles," she begged. "You have had as much to do with their upbringing as I have, you know."

At great length and in careful detail, he related their stories. He explained that the boys were neither angels, nor were they imps, and John was the more religious of the two. Both were excellent students. John, at twenty-two, would soon be graduating from Oxford with honors; Charles, at eighteen, equally gifted, would be entering Oxford. Both of them, he presumed, would in time be ordained priests in the Church of England, and would surely be used of the Lord in his vineyard. As for himself, Sammy planned to remain in the field of Christian education. As a student at Westminster he had become a King's Scholar, an honor which he proudly announced was being bestowed upon Charles as well.

At Oxford, Sammy had graduated with an M.A. from Christ Church, the same college to which

John had been elected at age seventeen. The older brother had had his share of disappointments; but he was a good man, and much success had been his to enjoy. He had helped his brothers as well as his parents financially from time to time, but he insisted that this be kept a secret. He was happily married, father to a son and a daughter. Susanna was justly proud of her first-born son.

Susanna's return to Wroot was anything but triumphant. In fact, the bad news she brought with her was only the beginning of more sorrows. The great patriarch of whom Samuel was writing would have had difficulty, himself, coping with the tribulations and reverses that fell upon the Wesleys in that one year, 1725.

First, the winter, which had been a hard one, left great banks of snow to melt and flood the area when the warm spring rain finally came in unusual abundance. Samuel was forced to make his trips to Epworth by boat. He rented a room there to preserve his waning strength.

Then Hetty wrote to her father, asking properly, for his approval of her engagement to a promising young lawyer. On the surface this sounded good. But Samuel, always cautious and more than a little suspicious of his daughter's suitors, sought to obtain a comprehensive resume of the man's character, and found little to commend him. He uncovered evidence that the prospective son-in-law was a dishonorable fellow, a woman chaser with a remarkably bad reputation.

The concerned father's letter of rejection, listing his reasons, succeeded only in angering the deeply infatuated daughter. She could believe nothing derogatory of her lover, and Samuel's letter probably arrived too late anyway. The sad story is that Hetty and her friend eloped and spent the night together, with plans to marry— so she was made to believe—in the morning of the morrow. To Hetty's dismay, her lawyer left her stranded.

She showed up eventually at the rectory in Wroot, a disillusioned, altogether unhappy young woman, to pour out her story in part to her despairing parents. Susanna, trying to place the best construction on the sordid situation, suggested that the man might have encountered trouble—an accident perhaps—and needed their help. She didn't sound convincing, even to herself.

"No, Mother." Hetty was weeping. "He's gone, and he left the trouble with me."

Poor girl. She desperately needed the love and compassion of an understanding father. But such behavior was not easily forgiven in the era (and the area) in which she lived. Samuel saw it as a failure on his part to be a perfect parent, the living precept and example of his preaching. Actually, his inability to forgive his daughter was an extension of his inability to forgive himself. He needed time; time to think, to meditate and pray; time to work out some kind of solution to the problem that appeared to be breaking down the moral fiber of the island, of which both he and Susanna had become justly proud.

He left the house without a word, which probably was a blessing. It gave Susanna time and opportunity to show her love for her daughter, to start with the existing situation and try to rebuild a life for her. Hetty relaxed in her mother's arms and wept until her tears were spent.

"I'll marry the first man who will have me under these circumstances," she said. "I will do everything I can to save the honor of the family, and I shall pray for my father's blessing." Even then, the end was not yet.

Samuel headed for Epworth, pulling frustratedly at the oars, attempting to dissipate the turmoil of his mind and spirit. Water splashed into the boat until his feet were soaked. Clouds gathered, and at about the halfway point, rain poured down upon him. Recurring chills told him he was going to be sick; so, in desperation, he turned the boat around and returned to Wroot. He took to his bed, with Susanna caring for him with such remedies as she knew, but they were not enough. He ran a fever for days, then began breaking out on his chest and face.

Smallpox! Another epidemic had reached the community. It was less severe than usual, but everyone in the family except Susanna contracted the dreaded malady. Samuel was slowly regaining his strength when he remarked to Susanna that if the Lord were trying to teach him a lesson, surely he had already learned it well. But there was more to come.

The poor man was stricken with paralysis. It was hardly a mild stroke, for it affected his arm and rendered his right hand numb and useless. But he didn't quit. There was something about his Irish blood that drove him on. Since he could no longer use his right hand to write, he immediately went about the task of teaching his left one to take over that responsibility; and he eventually succeeded.

Out of all these troubles, though, may have emerged a blessing in disguise. One day, while walking through the swamp to Epworth, Samuel bowed his head in humble submission to the "still small voice" of God. He stood amazed and rebuked to realize that, through the many months of his trials, not once had he spoken to a soul about the inward witness; and, more importantly, he could not remember having sensed its warm assurance within himself. The thought disturbed him deeply for, right or wrong, his Arminian theology held that one may lose the witness, and after preaching to others, might be cast away himself. He wasn't certain of the validity of this interpretation of the Word, for his father-in-law and friend, Dr. Annesley, had not agreed with him in this. But Samuel was much too conscientious to leave anything to chance. Quietly, soberly, reverently he renewed his covenant with God. And once again his faith, not only in his own salvation, but in the great awakening to come, was wonderfully restored.

It is hoped that, in his heart, he forgave his daughter Hetty who, still unmarried, was becoming heavy with child. Certainly he never condoned her sin. And while his attitude seemed harsh to the others of the family, it spoke volumes to the community, especially the church— where, for more than a quarter of a century, Sam had never compromised a principle nor glossed over any immoral act.

He approved and helped arrange her marriage to an illiterate tradesman who offered to take her as his wife and give his name to her unborn child. It was an answer to the problem, but the home was never a happy one.

Thus the winter passed, and just around the corner, a touch of spring appeared.

chapter **15**
The Inward Witness

In March 1726, John Wesley was highly honored at Oxford University, being elected a Fellow of Lincoln College. His father was ecstatic.

"Wherever I am, my Jack is a Fellow of Lincoln," he cried.

To become a Fellow at Oxford was more than an honor. Involved was an annual stipend and a suite of rooms reserved for the recipient that, when he was not on campus, could be rented to others. This financial benefit was especially rewarding to John, who was always short of funds. Out of his earnings he gave generous assistance to Charles, who had just entered Christ Church.

John was going home for the summer to assist his ailing father. Susanna, who worried about Samuel's health, could hardly have been more pleased. She made plans to have long talks with her son, and it turned out that those timely discussions were as beneficial to John as to his mother. He never forgot her sage advice.

In their first meeting, she asked him pointed questions regarding Charles.

"He's doing pretty well," John answered. "He was a bit bent on having a good time when he first arrived at Oxford, until we had some serious conversations. I understood him, for, of course, I have had my problems too, and I may have been a little stern. I remember one time he cried out facetiously, 'What! Would you have me be a saint all at once?' Recently, though, he has been doing much better."

"I'm glad," Susanna barely whispered. "You know, John, I have never been at ease after allowing him to be sent off to Westminster at the tender age of eight. I should have demanded that he be kept under my care for a few extra years at least. I'm afraid I failed him."

"Ah, my mother, quell your fears." John was wonderfully reassuring. "I received a letter from Charles soon after I arrived here." He took it from his pocket and read aloud the following excerpt; "'It is owing in great measure to somebody's prayers—my mother's, most likely—that I am come to think as I do; for I cannot tell myself how or when I woke out of my lethargy.'

"Charles resembles Father in many ways," John went on to explain. "He is emotional, optimistic, jovial, a talented speaker, and he is a good writer. His verses are first rate."

The following summer, 1727, Susanna could see that Samuel was failing, although he refused to admit it. Actually he was more concerned for Susanna's health than for his own. He wrote to John and Charles concerning the sudden illness their mother had developed, and they made a hurried journey home to be with her. She had pretty well recovered by the time of their arrival, but they saw a marked deterioration in their father. His trips across the swamp to Epworth were taking their toll, and the never-ending efforts to complete his *Dissertations on the Book of Job* were sapping his mental energy. John agreed to stay home and act as his curate, while Charles returned to his studies.

The dutiful John remained a year, preached twice each week, carried most of the pastoral load, and spent long hours in earnest conversation with his parents, making up for some of the time he had been separated from them.

His father pressed him to seek the inward witness, which John seemed unable to comprehend. Susanna exhorted him to live for the Lord, to keep all the laws of God with diligence. This he had always understood, but found impossible to put into practice as fully as he felt he ought to do. He kept such reservations hidden, however, and tried to compensate for them by admonishing Charles, through earnest correspondence, to live a holy life.

Charles, responding in kind, told his brother of a society he and some like-minded friends had organized that some of the students were calling "The Holy Club." He went on to say that they lived—to the best of their ability—by a long list of virtues to which were being added new, more stringent statutes as they came to light. He added that self-examination, such as their mother had always contended for, was a daily exercise with each of them.

John was elated as he read the letter to his parents. Samuel was pleased and stated calmly that surely no one could object to such well-disciplined living. Susanna's "cup was running over." She felt certain her prayers were being answered. Surely her sons were teaching the principles and practicing the precepts for which she had contended and struggled since the days of her childhood.

When John returned to Oxford, he found the men deeply involved in the project Charles had described in his letters. The fellowship, however, was so loosely knit, with differences of opinion retarding its progress, that the meticulous John despaired of its future. That is, until by unanimous vote, he became the leader of the club. He accepted the challenge, perfected the organization, and soon the highly disciplined, devout young adherents were nicknamed "Methodists" by their fellows at Oxford.

That year, John Wesley was ordained a priest in the Anglican Church.

A new sorrow befell the Wesleys. Sam and Susanna had once befriended a poor young man in Wroot whose name was John Whitelamb. John was a homely young fellow, lean of face and frame, but possessed of an agile mind and a heart of gold. Susanna had taken him under her care, teaching him faithfully. He became secretary to Samuel, assisting him with his work on Job. Finally, with considerable sacrifice, they helped support him through Oxford, where son John had become his tutor without pay. Following graduation the young man returned to Wroot, where he served well as curate to Samuel.

In due course, to everyone's surprise, John Whitelamb and Mary Wesley fell madly in love. Mary's pretty face and sunny disposition outweighed her tragically crippled body in the eyes of her adoring suitor. They were happily wed.

Since travel between Samuel's two points had become so difficult, the Wesleys had moved back to Epworth. So the work at Wroot was given to their new son-in-law. Hardly could John and Mary have been happier as they moved into the rectory to begin their life together. Several months later their joy was made complete with Mary's announcement that a child was on the way.

But poor Mary's twisted body, which had denied her many of the common blessings of life, could not endure the pregnancy. She and the baby both died. John remained single and served the church at Wroot for many years. The beautiful influence of Mary's unselfish life and untimely death lived on, working its own miracles.

Samuel's health continued to deteriorate, although he still would not admit it, even after being involved in an accident which might have taken his life. It happened one day when he and Susanna were riding in the back of a wagon. The horses shied and began to run, throwing him over the side and onto the hard ground. The heavy back wheel barely missed him as it passed. Neighbors working nearby stopped the horses and carefully laid Sam's bruised and bleeding body onto the wagon-bed and took him home. Susanna, who had nearly been thrown from the wagon too, held his head in her lap and prayed as they bounced along over the rough terrain. Fortunately, he sustained no broken bones, but he never recovered fully from the shock of the fall. Even so, he continued his ministerial duties, apparently unaware that he was failing to perform at his former level of efficiency.

With the passing of many months, though, he began to sense the seriousness of his situation, and two great fears possessed him. One was that he might not live to complete his *Dissertations on the Book of Job;* the other, related to the first, was a deep concern for Susanna's future following his decease, when another minister would be assigned to the church at Epworth.

It was with wishful thinking that he wrote to Samuel, Jr., offering to resign his post in the younger man's favor, thus assuring Susanna a life of comfort in the house she knew so well. Could it be that the aging rector had forgotten there is more to the divine call than convenience? Sammy was more than willing to provide a home for his mother when she needed it, but he was not about to leave the city to go live in Lincolnshire.

Samuel wrote to John (who loved Epworth) offering him the same proposition. John gave serious consideration to the suggestion, but finally decided against it. He too, of course, would gladly assist his mother in her hour of need.

Where was Susanna during these deliberations on her behalf? Much of the time she was in her room, reading, meditating, praying; petitioning God to supply whatever needs she would have, both temporally and in the world to come. Characteristically, she neither smiled nor frowned, but remained her pleasant self.

Her deep concern for Samuel is a matter of record. In a letter to John, she wrote, "Your father is in a bad state of health: he sleeps little and eats less. He seems not to have any apprehension of his approaching exit, but I fear he has only a short time to live. It is with much pain and difficulty that he performs Divine Service on the Lord's Day. Everybody observes his decay but himself. . . ."

Her deep, abiding love for him was manifesting itself anew. When he announced that he was going to make one last trip to London, particularly to oversee the publishing of his book and seek permission to dedicate it to the Queen, Susanna was deeply disturbed. But happily, he accomplished both objectives.

Sam returned to Epworth, calling upon the last of his waning strength; and, with the advent of winter 1734, he took to his bed for the last time. As his condition worsened, the family began to gather. To the surprise of everyone, it was Susanna—always brave and calm in times of trouble—who seemed unable to face the fact of Samuel's approaching departure. Feelings of guilt possessed her. She entertained a fear that, upon occasion, she had reacted to Sam's impracticality with a less than loving attitude. She had never doubted his love, for even during those tense times he had remained kind and optimistic.

Three times, as Samuel neared the end, Susanna asked her sons to go with her to his side. On each occasion, she was overcome with deep emotions that had never found satisfactory release. Attempting to look down into his dimming eyes, she experienced an inexplicable loss of strength and crumpled to the floor. She would gladly have laid down her life for his, the only man she had ever loved.

The end was drawing near. Samuel asked for Charles, who came and sat by the side of his father's bed. In that final conversation, the dying man described again that great awakening he believed the Lord had given him a vision of many years before.

"My son," he said, "above all else be patient.

Be steady. The Christian faith will surely revive in this kingdom; you shall see it, though I shall not."

"Yes, Father, I'll pray every morning of my life for just such an outpouring of the Spirit as I have heard you describe. I remember hearing you cry out for revival when I was a little boy."

Samuel seemed to relax; the effort to converse had tired him. He closed his eyes and slept. For a moment, Charles feared his father was slipping away, but his steady breathing assured the son that the end was not yet. The young man prayed, telling the Lord, in effect, that nothing he could see at the moment, save his father's faith indicated any hope of revival amid the spiritual and moral decline around him. But there was something strangely contagious about his parent's faith, and he told the Lord about that too, promising to be patient and steady as his father had exhorted him.

A few moments later, Samuel awoke. "I'll go now, Father," Charles said as he arose from his chair. "I don't wish to tire you any more."

"Getting tired doesn't matter now, my son. Please ask John to come in." And Samuel closed his eyes again.

John entered his father's room and the two talked briefly, but Samuel kept drifting off to sleep. Then, sensing his son was about to leave, the feeble man forced himself to attention. Laying his crippled hand upon a slender wrist, he cried out with unusual strength "John, my John!"

"Yes, Father."

"The inward witness, son, the inward witness. That is the proof, the strongest proof of Christianity!"

"I shall remember that, Father. I will seek it, and 'He that seeketh, findeth.' "

John pressed his father's hand and quietly left the room, but he was troubled in soul. He hadn't really believed the words he spoke in an effort to comfort the dying man he loved. Later, he discussed the problem with his mother, saying, "I'm taking your advice; it's all I know to do. Someday, I hope to live well enough that I shall know I'm ready to meet my Lord."

Susanna gave him her blessing.

Samuel Wesley died in perfect peace at three score years and ten, plus two. In a most appropriate, solemn ceremony, he was laid to rest beside the Epworth church. A large flat monument bearing the following inscription, written by Susanna, marks his grave:

> Here lyeth all that was mortal of Samuel Wesley, A.M. He was rector of Epworth 39 years, and departed this life 25th of April, 1735, aged 72: And as he lived so he died in the True Catholic faith of the Holy Trinity in Unity and that Jesus Christ is God Incarnate; and the only Saviour of mankind, Acts IV,12.

> Blessed are the dead which die in the Lord, yea saith the spirit that they may rest from

> their labours and their works do follow
> them. Rev. XIV,13.

Sammy was assisting his brothers in settling their father's affairs. The rector had lived just long enough to know that his two great earthly ambitions were finally to be realized. For the first time in nearly forty years, his debts would be paid in full, and his monumental work on the book of Job, already published, would be earning royalties.

Everything—machinery, animals, household goods—was sold to make way for the incoming pastor. There was little enough left for Susanna—much less than Samuel had projected—and the sale of his book was disappointing. But the one lady in his life was left with riches greater than gold. Hers was the profound respect and love of her family and a great host of friends. Nothing in all the records suggests that any of her children resented the disciplined life she had pressed upon them, or blamed her in any measure for the poverty they endured. She had not one enemy in all the world, and that was wealth enough to sustain her.

Susanna was fighting tears as she walked out the door of the rectory where she had spent more than half her life; but no one knew it except herself. She left with head held high, beautiful in mourning; her steps were firm and steadfast. She neither smiled nor frowned, and no one could have guessed that powerful emotions were trying their best to surface.

Her sons and daughters were leaving, returning to their own abodes. Sammy, who by then
was living at Tiverton, took Kezzie with him and
made a home for her. Martha was living with
her Uncle Matthew in London. At least two of
the other girls resided in the city too.

Emily insisted upon her mother sharing her
home in Gainsborough, where she kept a private
school. This proved to be an excellent arrangement, for it gave Susanna an opportunity to be of
assistance and to feel needed. John and Charles
returned to Oxford.

chapter *16*
"Sing a Psalm of Praise"

Two months had passed since Samuel's death, and Susanna's grief was subsiding. She was happily situated, living with Emily. With time on her hands, she gave herself to the writing of letters. No longer was she burdened with the problems of finding food for her family, caring for the sick, working the glebe, and facing unending indebtedness. While she never ceased to mourn for many departed loved ones, including her brother in India, her shattered hopes for financial security in her old age bothered her no more. She said, "I am induced to believe that it is much easier to be contented without riches than with them."

Yet she was not as personally contented as might have been expected. For the first time in her life, she was beginning to question her own theology. She thought about Samuel, recalling mostly his good qualities. How she missed him! "If only I had questioned him pointedly concerning the inward witness which he claimed as proof of his salvation, perhaps my joy would be full," she told herself. She wanted to discuss all this with Emily. But how could she, having ignored the matter through all the years she had lived and labored with her husband?

Adding weight to her problem was her realization that John and Charles were troubled also. Their radically disciplined lives, which they (and she) believed approached perfection, were still without that "peace of God that passeth understanding." Their letters told her so. She couldn't help noting that they, too, carefully avoided any reference to their father's final admonition to John. Susanna wondered whether they, like herself, would now give everything for just one opportunity to discuss with him that "strongest proof of Christianity." Could it be that she had erred in spending her life without asking what God could do for her; thinking only of what she could do for him? Were her boys struggling with a problem she had pressed upon them? She wondered. *There is one thing certain*, she mused. *Old age is the worst time we can choose to mend either our lives or our fortunes.*

On the table lay a letter from Martha that should have made Susanna supremely happy. It read simply that she was marrying an Anglican clergyman named Westley Hall. Her Uncle Matthew approved the match, which was to be solemnized at his London home. "Soon," Martha went on to say, "we will be moving into the rectory at Wooton."

But a message from her son Sammy, which arrived in the same post, disturbed Susanna. Sammy, like his father, had always been an excellent judge of men. He was acquainted with this man, Hall, the letter read, and he didn't trust him. He had reason to suspect that he was morally weak, unstable, and that Martha, like too many of his sisters, was headed for heartache.

Susanna bowed in prayer, beseeching heaven that, this time, Sammy's judgment would be in error. As it happened, Martha and her husband spent many good years together in the ministry. Sammy must have had some basis for his fears, however, for eventually Westley Hall did run into trouble—but neither Sammy nor his mother lived to see it.

Susanna had kept in close touch with Sammy from the day he left the rectory at Epworth, needing one, at least, in her family who was successful, dependable, and strong. She had always admired his stern, stable disposition. He lived well, but he lacked the warm glow of his mother's pleasing personality. Sammy was a loyal churchman who gave no credence to the emotional, mystical qualities of evangelicalism, and this sentiment expressed itself in a further note of disapproval in his letter.

There was a rumor abroad, it said, that John

and Charles were contemplating a missionary journey to America, hoping that, in converting the natives, they might save their own souls. This, according to Sammy, was pure rubbish. "Why, under heaven," he asked, "should such fine young men who have been properly baptized, educated, and indoctrinated in the church, be struggling for that upon which no one can lay a hand?"

Susanna hadn't heard about those plans, but in the next post a letter from John assured her that the story was more than idle gossip. General Oglethorpe, it said, was assembling a group of emigrants bound for the New World. Among them were persecuted Protestants seeking religious freedom, including a large number of Moravian Brethren from Germany who were well known for their piety and evangelistic fervor. John had been asked to go along as the ship's chaplain; Charles was being offered the position of secretary to the general. It was plain that both men were anxious for an opportunity to evangelize the Indians, which their father had often expressed a desire to do. John went on to say, however, that he felt keenly his responsibility to his mother, and neither he nor Charles would go without her full approval.

They got it. "Had I twenty sons," she wrote, "I should rejoice that they were all so employed, though I should never see them more."

Before John and Charles embarked on what was to be a most disappointing missionary venture across the sea, Emily accepted a proposal of marriage. Twice before she had been so engaged, but both times family pressures, brought mostly by her brother Sammy, had induced her to terminate the romances. Now, at forty-four, she could hardly be blamed for asking no one's advice as she entered into matrimony; but it did not turn out to be a happy union.

Susanna went to live with Sammy and his wife at Tiverton. Kezzie, by then, was staying with the Halls at Wooton.

It was to Sammy's door, one bitter day in December 1736, that a dejected, disappointed, spiritually defeated Charles Wesley made a surprise appearance. He had failed completely, both as secretary to General Oglethorpe and as a missionary to the Indians.

Sammy could have said, "I told you so," but he didn't, for Charles had always been his favorite sibling. He welcomed the young man home with everything except the "fatted calf," and made the reunion a pleasant time indeed for their mother.

Susanna was worried about John, who had remained abroad. Charles' account of the New World venture was unduly harsh and prejudiced. It wasn't that Susanna didn't believe his stories, but she was convinced there was more to be told. She accepted in minute detail, though, Charles' vivid account of a storm at sea on the way to America. She sensed that it could hardly have been imagined.

"Both John and I were in disfavor with the passengers," Charles admitted. "We tried to press our Holy Club discipline upon them. The Moravians were professing a high state of grace, but since they didn't live as well as we believed they should, they considered us bigots and we looked upon them as hypocrites. The breach was widening when a storm, a veritable typhoon that I have not words to describe, came upon us. Thunder, lightning, blackened skies, raging winds, and turbulent waters tossed the tiny bark at will, until not one soul aboard held any hope of surviving. It seemed that the very next swell would swallow us completely and carry us to the bottom of the sea. Such wailing and screaming, I think, will never be heard again this side of perdition. Both John and I were terrified beyond anything I can tell you. We didn't dare to die. Our good works were as filthy rags; we were lost and we knew it. Then, to our utter amazement, we heard those Moravian Brethren singing Psalms and praising God. It was plain to see they welcomed death as an open door to heaven. We fell on our faces and called out to God to save our lives. It was as though we had no right to ask him to save our souls."

He paused and Susanna saw his body shake with a tremor as he recalled the raging tempest. She laid her hand upon his and said, "It's all right now, son. God must have answered your prayers, for he did save your lives. You believe that, don't you?"

"Yes, Mother, but I'm utterly confused. John and I both preach *saving faith*, but neither of us have it. I wonder if we should ever preach again."

Susanna could only ponder these things in her heart.

The privilege of spending time with her children brought real comfort and joy to Susanna. She went next to Wooton to live for several months with Martha and Westley Hall. It was there that John came to see her, when he too arrived back in England earlier than was originally intended. He and his mother profited greatly through long talks together, leaning heavily upon one another for badly needed strength and courage.

John, of course, gave his version of the missionary venture across the sea. "You must keep in mind," he said, "that America is new territory; a culture different from anything we know. It is inhabited with rugged men and women, and our success there in evangelizing the natives or anyone else, was little enough. Even so, Charles did much better as Christ's preacher than as General Oglethorpe's secretary. I was forced, finally, to take over his duties, and this, of course, was not easy on his pride.

"I'm sure he told you of the storm at sea. We are both convinced the Moravians enjoy an inward witness of the Spirit which we have not received. One of their leaders, Peter Bohler, is being most helpful to Charles and me, and we are searching the Scriptures daily, hoping to find that peace which Jesus promised his people. We have been distressed by the knowledge that we have never found the faith for ourselves which we preach to others and we would have given up if it were not for Peter Bohler. He says we should preach faith till we have it; then, because we have it, we will preach faith. We are acting on his advice."

John was unable to interpret his mother's reaction to what he was saying. She showed interest, to be sure, but her pleasant, unsmiling response was noncommittal. Whether she was pleased or bored was anybody's guess.

Months rolled by, then three important bits of news filtered through to Sammy, hence to Susanna and the others of the family:

First, Charles, on a bed of sickness, had "touched the hem of the garment." His faith had made him whole. ("Oh, for a thousand tongues to sing. . . .")

Second, John, taking courage from his brother's testimony, had gone to a meeting one night in Aldersgate Street where, according to his confession, his "heart was strangely warmed." He wrote in his journal, "I did trust in Christ, Christ alone, for salvation; and an assurance was given me that he had taken away my sins, even mine, and saved me from the law of sin and death."

Third, suddenly John and Charles were preaching with nearly unprecedented fervor and effectiveness, bringing people by scores to the place of repentance. But some of the converts—poor people released from the bonds of sin and rebellion—were given to excitement, enthusiasm, and demonstration—both in and out of the Spirit, no doubt—which was invoking harsh criticism upon themselves, the preachers, and the revival.

"Scandalous!" shouted Sammy. But stronger adjectives than that found their way into his letters to Susanna. She, as a loving mother, held her peace.

Then John paid his mother a visit to present his case himself, and she appeared to retain an open mind.

George Whitefield, an enthusiastic member of the Holy Club (and purported to be the most powerful preacher of the day), called upon her too, answering questions she might not have asked her sons.

The revival spread swiftly, and the criticism became more and more intense. The fiery evangelists were soon denied the privilege of preaching in the churches; so—Whitefield first, then the Wesleys—reluctantly took to the fields. In a matter of weeks, multitudes were gathering in out-of-door meetings from London to Bristol and beyond, and thousands were converted.

Susanna was plainly perplexed. Sammy's letters continued to condemn the movement as nothing but wild fanaticism. Martha and Westley Hall remained neutral, neither promoting nor opposing the revival, while becoming deeply concerned for Susanna. She was spending her days alone in her room. They could hear her praying, but could only guess the substance of her petitions and the burden of her heart.

Actually, she was confused. Her cries were for light and direction from heaven. She was impressed by the results of the awakening, which she couldn't deny. Sinners, just like the ones she had spent a lifetime trying to reform, were suddenly being transformed into Bible-believing soldiers of the cross. Keeping the Commandments for the pure joy of serving the Savior, they were taking the "way" without a quibble. At the evening meal on Saturday she hardly spoke a word to her loved ones, and afterward returned quickly to her room.

Sunday morning she sat in the church with Martha, and together they knelt for Communion. Westley Hall was serving the elements, and as he passed the cup to Susanna, she was a picture of bleak despair. Then, as he repeated the words, "The blood of our Lord Jesus Christ which was given for thee . . ." she visibly relaxed; and light, a lovely, heavenly light as beautiful as the first rays of dawn, glowed from her features. A new name—and a precious one indeed—was written down in glory.

Any display of emotion would not have been in character with Susanna. Neither could there be any visible change in life-style, since she had walked according to the ordinances of God for more than sixty long and difficult years. Her witnessing words, as might be expected, were simple and direct. Referring to the Communion rite, she said: "Those words struck through to my heart, and I knew that God for Christ's sake had forgiven me all my sins."

In all the years of the revival, no testimonial could possibly have thrilled the hearts of John and Charles Wesley as did those simple words spoken by their mother. They were careful, however, to pay no elaborate attention to her "eleventh hour" spiritual experience, in response to her own wishes, which were well founded.

When her spiritual eyes were opened, she visualized truth from the perspective of a long life lived for God. Most new Christians begin a process of growth in grace and knowledge from a point low on the spiritual ladder. Susanna, in her moment of transformation, was made great in grace, for her knowledge of God's will and her dedication to his cause had so long been a matter of record.

A whole new concept of truth simply opened before her. Unlike most adult converts, she didn't regret having failed in her youth to accept Christ through faith. She was convinced that both she and her husband had been used of God, according to his will, throughout their lives together. During that darkest hour, just before the dawning of revival, the necessity of faith and works as a team in harness was being epitomized in them, hence to be practiced and preached by their progeny. Now Samuel's final prophetic words to Charles: "The Christian faith will surely revive in this kingdom; you shall see it, though I will not," were already coming true.

Whether it was Susanna who told John of the deserted foundry near Bunnhill Fields is not known. What is known is that John did indeed purchase the property and made of the building a chapel with living quarters above. And it was there that Susanna lived and labored the last three years of her life. Not only was she a loyal supporter of the revival, but nowhere could John have found a more spiritual, knowledgeable, level-headed advisor to direct him. It was she who impressed upon him the necessity of discarding his High Church prejudices and applying new methods to meet the needs of the growing, glowing revival which was already moving beyond the borders of Britain.

And it was there, with that "peace of God that passeth all understanding," that Susanna Wesley lay dying at the age of seventy-three. Surrounded by her daughters and John, who read the commendatory prayer, she made one last request: "Please, my children, as soon as I am released, sing a psalm of praise to God."

Susanna Annesley Wesley was laid to rest in Bunnhill Fields on August 1, 1742, to await the resurrection dawn. On a plain stone marker the following verses, written by Charles, were carefully inscribed:

In sure and steadfast hope to rise,
And claim her mansion in the skies,
A Christian here her flesh laid down,
The cross exchanging for a crown.

True daughter of affliction, she,
Inured to pain and misery,
Mourn'd a long night of griefs and fears,
A legal night of seventy years.

The Father then reveal'd his Son,
Him in the broken bread made known,
She knew and felt her sins forgiven,
And found the earnest of her heaven.

Meet for the fellowship above,
She heard the call, "Arise, my love!"
"I come," her dying looks replied,
And lamb-like, as her Lord, she died.

Other Living Books Best-sellers

THE ANGEL OF HIS PRESENCE by Grace Livingston Hill. This book captures the romance of John Wentworth Stanley and a beautiful young woman whose influence causes John to reevaluate his well-laid plans for the future. 07-0047 $2.95.

ANSWERS by Josh McDowell and Don Stewart. In a question-and-answer format, the authors tackle sixty-five of the most-asked questions about the Bible, God, Jesus Christ, miracles, other religions, and creation. 07-0021 $3.95.

THE BEST CHRISTMAS PAGEANT EVER by Barbara Robinson. A delightfully wild and funny story about what happens to a Christmas program when the "Horrible Herdman" brothers and sisters are miscast in the roles of the biblical Christmas story characters. 07-0137 $2.50.

BUILDING YOUR SELF-IMAGE by Josh McDowell. Here are practical answers to help you overcome your fears, anxieties, and lack of self-confidence. Learn how God's higher image of who you are can take root in your heart and mind. 07-1395 $3.95.

THE CHILD WITHIN by Mari Hanes. The author shares insights she gained from God's Word during her own pregnancy. She identifies areas of stress, offers concrete data about the birth process, and points to God's sure promises that he will "gently lead those that are with young." 07-0219 $2.95.

400 WAYS TO SAY I LOVE YOU by Alice Chapin. Perhaps the flame of love has almost died in your marriage. Maybe you have a good marriage that just needs a little "spark." Here is a book especially for the woman who wants to rekindle the flame of romance in her marriage; who wants creative, practical, useful ideas to show the man in her life that she cares. 07-0919 $2.95.

GIVERS, TAKERS, AND OTHER KINDS OF LOVERS by Josh McDowell and Paul Lewis. This book bypasses vague generalities about love and sex and gets right to the basic questions: Whatever happened to sexual freedom? What's true love like? Do men respond differently than women? If you're looking for straight answers about God's plan for love and sexuality, this book was written for you. 07-1031 $2.95.

HINDS' FEET ON HIGH PLACES by Hannah Hurnard. A classic allegory of a journey toward faith that has sold more than a million copies! 07-1429 $3.95.

HOW TO BE HAPPY THOUGH MARRIED by Tim LaHaye. One of America's most successful marriage counselors gives practical, proven advice for marital happiness. 07-1499 $3.50.

JOHN, SON OF THUNDER by Ellen Gunderson Traylor. In this saga of adventure, romance, and discovery, travel with John—the disciple whom Jesus loved—down desert paths, through the courts of the Holy City, to the foot of the cross. Journey with him from his luxury as a privileged son of Israel to the bitter hardship of his exile on Patmos. 07-1903 $4.95.

Other Living Books Best-sellers

KAREN'S CHOICE by Janice Hermansen. College students Karen and Jon fall in love and are heading toward marriage when Karen discovers she is pregnant. Struggle with Karen and Jon through the choices they make and observe how they cope with the consequences and eventually find the forgiveness of Christ. 07-2027 $3.50.

LIFE IS TREMENDOUS! by Charlie "Tremendous" Jones. Believing that enthusiasm makes the difference, Jones shows how anyone can be happy, involved, relevant, productive, healthy, and secure in the midst of a high-pressure, commercialized society. 07-2184 $2.95.

LOOKING FOR LOVE IN ALL THE WRONG PLACES by Joe White. Using wisdom gained from many talks with young people, White steers teens in the right direction to find love and fulfillment in a personal relationship with God. 07-3825 $3.50.

LORD, COULD YOU HURRY A LITTLE? by Ruth Harms Calkin. These prayer-poems from the heart of a godly woman trace the inner workings of the heart, following the rhythms of the day and the seasons of the year with expectation and love. 07-3816 $2.95.

LORD, I KEEP RUNNING BACK TO YOU by Ruth Harms Calkin. In prayer-poems tinged with wonder, joy, humanness, and questioning, the author speaks for all of us who are groping and learning together what it means to be God's child. 07-3819 $3.50.

LORD, YOU LOVE TO SAY YES by Ruth Harms Calkin. In this collection of prayer-poems the author speaks openly and honestly with her Lord about hopes and dreams, longings and frustrations, and her observations of life. 07-3824 $3.50.

MORE THAN A CARPENTER by Josh McDowell. A hard-hitting book for people who are skeptical about Jesus' deity, his resurrection, and his claims on their lives. 07-4552 $2.95.

MOUNTAINS OF SPICES by Hannah Hurnard. Here is an allegory comparing the nine spices mentioned in the Song of Solomon to the nine fruits of the Spirit. A story of the glory of surrender by the author of *HINDS' FEET ON HIGH PLACES*. 07-4611 $3.95.

THE NEW MOTHER'S BOOK OF BABY CARE by Marjorie Palmer and Ethel Bowman. From when to call the doctor to what you will need to clothe the baby, this book will give you all the basic knowledge necessary to be the parent your child needs. 07-4695 $2.95.

NOW IS YOUR TIME TO WIN by Dave Dean. In this true-life story, Dean shares how he locked into seven principles that enabled him to bounce back from failure to success. Read about successful men and women—from sports and entertainment celebrities to the ordinary people next door—and discover how you too can bounce back from failure to success! 07-4727 $2.95.

THE POSITIVE POWER OF JESUS CHRIST by Norman Vincent Peale. All his life the author has been leading men and women to Jesus Christ. In this book he tells of his boyhood encounters with Jesus and of his spiritual growth as he attended seminary and began his world-renowned ministry. 07-4914 $3.95.

Other Living Books Best-sellers

REASONS by Josh McDowell and Don Stewart. In a convenient question-and-answer format, the authors address many of the commonly asked questions about the Bible and evolution. 07-5287 $3.95.

ROCK by Bob Larson. A well-researched and penetrating look at today's rock music and rock performers, their lyrics, and their life-styles. 07-5686 $3.50.

SHAPE UP FROM THE INSIDE OUT by John R. Throop. Learn how to conquer the problem of being overweight! In this honest, often humorous book, Throop shares his own personal struggle with this area and how he gained fresh insight about the biblical relationship between physical and spiritual fitness. 07-5899 $2.95.

SUCCESS: THE GLENN BLAND METHOD by Glenn Bland. The author shows how to set goals and make plans that really work. His ingredients of success include spiritual, financial, educational, and recreational balances. 07-6689 $3.50.

TAKE ME HOME by Bonnie Jamison. This touching, candid story of the author's relationship with her dying mother will offer hope and assurance to those dealing with an aging parent, relative, or friend. 07-6901 $3.50.

TELL ME AGAIN, LORD, I FORGET by Ruth Harms Calkin. You will easily identify with Calkin in this collection of prayer-poems about the challenges, peaks, and quiet moments of each day. 07-6990 $3.50.

THROUGH GATES OF SPLENDOR by Elisabeth Elliot. This unforgettable story of five men who braved the Auca Indians has become one of the most famous missionary books of all times. 07-7151 $3.95.

WAY BACK IN THE HILLS by James C. Hefley. The story of Hefley's colorful childhood in the Ozarks makes reflective reading for those who like a nostalgic journey into the past. 07-7821 $3.95.

WHAT WIVES WISH THEIR HUSBANDS KNEW ABOUT WOMEN by James Dobson. The best-selling author of *DARE TO DISCIPLINE* and *THE STRONG-WILLED CHILD* brings us this vital book that speaks to the unique emotional needs and aspirations of today's woman. An immensely practical, interesting guide. 07-7896 $3.50.

YES by Ann Kiemel. In this window into Ann's heart, she tells—in her usual honest, charming way—how she has answered a resounding YES to Jesus in the various circumstances of her life. 07-8563 $2.95.

The books listed are available at your bookstore. If unavailable, send check with order to cover retail price plus $1.00 per book for postage and handling to:

Tyndale DMS
Box 80
Wheaton, Illinois 60189

Prices and availability subject to change without notice. Allow 4–6 weeks for delivery.